DISCARDED

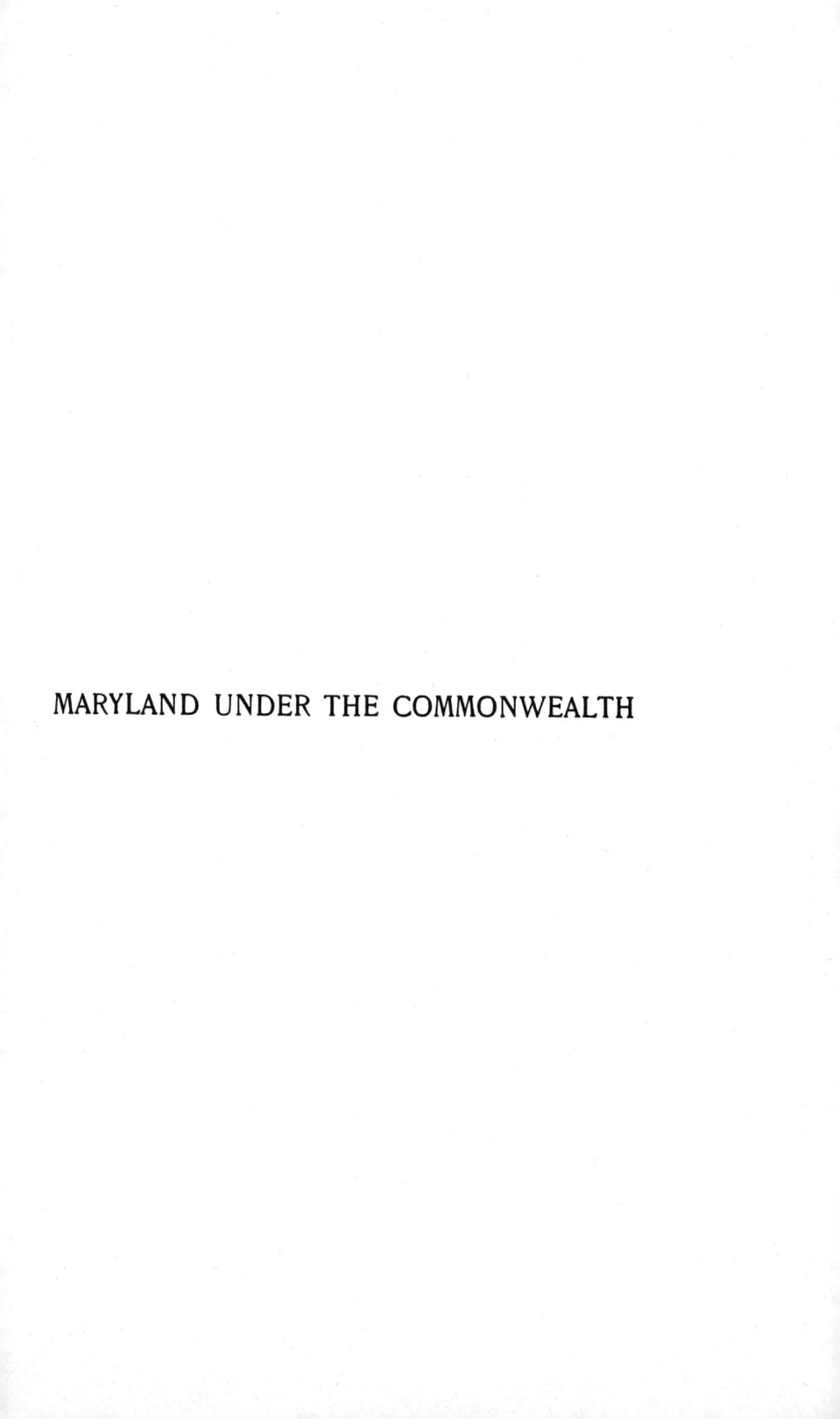

MARYLAND UNDER THE COMMONWEALTH

SERIES XXIX NO. 1

JOHNS HOPKINS UNIVERSITY STUDIES
IN
HISTORICAL AND POLITICAL SCIENCE

Under the Direction of the

Departments of History, Political Economy, and
Political Science

MARYLAND UNDER THE COMMONWEALTH

A CHRONICLE OF THE YEARS 1649-1658

BY

BERNARD C. STEINER, PH.D.
Associate in English Historical Jurisprudence

AMS PRESS
NEW YORK

Reprinted from the edition of 1911, Baltimore

First AMS EDITION published 1971

Manufactured in the United States of America

International Standard Book Number :0-404-06248-2

Library of Congress Catalog Number: 79-158209

AMS PRESS INC.
NEW YORK, N.Y. 10003

CONTENTS.

	PAGE.
Preface	vii
I. Provincial Conditions in 1649–50	9
II. The Assembly of 1650	17
III. Proprietor and Colonists, 1650–1	36
IV. The Proprietor's Instructions of 1651	48
V. The Commissioners of Parliament of 1651	53
VI. The Proprietor's Struggle in England to Retain his Province	61
VII. Governor Stone, 1652–3	65
VIII. Stone's Breach with the Commissioners, 1654	72
IX. The Maryland Civil War, 1654	84
X. Conditions after the War	101
XI. Josias Fendall, Governor, 1656	106
XII. Restoration of Proprietary Government, 1657	112

APPENDIX

Proceedings of the Provincial Courts, 1649 to 1658, Chronologically Arranged ... 117

PREFACE.

The study here presented differs from the historical monographs usually published in this series, in that, instead of the development of a single theme in Maryland history, it offers a chronological view of a short period. The object is to present in as complete a manner as possible the facts on record relating to the years 1649 to 1658. This period has not been studied in detail since the publication of the corresponding volumes of the Maryland Archives, the Calvert Papers, and the Maryland Historical Magazine. The paper will, therefore, serve as a compendious record of established testimony. Appended is a summary of cases decided and matters considered in the Provincial Court. The nature of the controversies, the mixture of trivial and serious concerns which came before the chief judicial tribunal, throw light upon the occupations and welfare of the colony.

Similar accounts of earlier periods of Maryland history have been published in these Studies as follows: Beginnings of Maryland, 1631-1639, Series XXI, Nos. 8-10; Maryland during the English Civil Wars, Part I, Series XXIV, Nos. 11-12; Part II, Series XXV, Nos. 4-5.

MARYLAND UNDER THE COMMONWEALTH.

I. Provincial Conditions in 1649-50.

The year 1649 opens a distinct period in the history of the Province of Maryland. William Stone had come from the Eastern Shore of Virginia to be Governor, and with him, doubtless partly at his solicitation, came a number of settlers destined to bring a new religious and political influence into the Province. The legislature had just passed the famous toleration act, placing in permanent form what had been the policy of the Proprietary from the beginning of his colony. The coming of new settlers was shortly to lead to the formation of two new counties and to do away with the conditions existing when there were only two centres, St. Mary's and Kent Island. The fall of the monarchy in England placed new influences in control there, which must be reckoned with, and the colonists, as always, were eagerly looking to the mother-country for countenance in their acts. A Protestant Governor in the Province had to satisfy a Roman Catholic Proprietary and a Puritan Commonwealth in England. Such were conditions when spring came in 1649.

A Congregational, or Independent, church had been formed in Virginia in 1642, and had the benefit of a New England clergyman for a time.[1] In spite of the laws of that

---

[1] Beverly, History and Present State of Virginia, 51, 229. Burk, History of Virginia, II, 67, 75. Holmes, Annals of America, I, 198, 321. Bozman, History of Maryland, II, 370, 373. Hall, The Lords Baltimore and the Maryland Palatinate, 54. They sent to New England for ministers in 1642. In 1643 Virginia passed an act ordering nonconformists to leave the Province with all conveniency. Neill, English Colonization of America during the Seventeenth Century, 278 ff., on Dr. Thomas Harrison and the Virginia Puritans. Hawks, Early History of the Southern States, 57. Neill, Virginia Carolorum, 165 ff. Neill, Founders of Maryland, 116. Davis, The Day-Star of American Freedom, 68 ff.

9

colony against dissenters, which had begun in 1639, "though as yet none" lived in the Province, this church had so increased as to be said to number one hundred and eighteen members in 1648. In the latter year Sir William Berkeley determined on a more rigid enforcement of the laws for conformity and broke up the church. The members of the organization dispersed: Thomas Harrison, the pastor, went to Boston toward the end of the year, and William Durand, the elder, Richard Bennett, and a number of others came to Maryland. It is quite probable that the bringing of these Puritans to the Province was the inducement named in Stone's commission as the reason for his appointment as Governor. During the whole of the year 1649 they were coming into Maryland, and they made their settlement, calling it Providence, on the west side of the Chesapeake, above St. Mary's and near the mouth of the Severn River.[1] Probably their hamlet stood upon what is now Greenberry's Point, and there may have been three hundred settlers in all.[2]

No government appears to have been established over this settlement by the Provincial authorities before the summer of 1650, and Bozman's conjecture is quite probable that, as all the settlers were members of the same church, the church authorities, headed by Durand, kept the people in order. Though many have thought that Baltimore's officers invited the Puritans, Leonard Strong, one of their own number, expressly denied this,[3] and John Langford, writing on the Proprietary side in the controversy, says that they were only "received and protected."[4] Hammond, in "Leah and Rachel," says that the Puritans courted Maryland as a

[1] D. R. Randall, A Puritan Colony in Maryland (Johns Hopkins University Studies in Historical and Political Science, Series 4, Number 6, pp. 17, 19). R. H. Williams estimated the number at from five to eight hundred. J. W. Randall, Address in Hall of House of Delegates at Invitation of Mayor and Council of Annapolis on 250th Anniversary of Passage of Act Concerning Religion, 12, 16. Davis, 68, but see Ridgely, Annals of Annapolis, 33.
[2] Davis, 83. Sixty tracts of land in St. Mary's County have prefix St. and only three in Anne Arundel County (Davis, 150).
[3] Babylon's Fall in Maryland. See below, p. 85.
[4] A Just and Cleere Refutation of a false and scandalous Pamphlet Entituled Babylon's Fall in Maryland. See below, p. 86.

refuge: "their conditions were pitied, their propositions were hearkened to," that they "should have convenient portions of land assigned them, liberty of conscience and privilege to choose their own officers and hold courts within themselves, all was granted. They had a whole county of the richest land in the Province assigned them." Each one was granted land according to the Conditions of Plantation, which were common to all adventurers. Richard Bennett, who was a merchant, seems to have resided but little in Maryland. In August, 1650, he claimed that debts were owed him by Copley and other Marylanders for goods and that Lewger's house and property in the Province had been transferred to him.[1] He appointed Hatton his attorney for the collection of these debts, and conveyed to John Lewger, Jr., his father's house and land, subject to Hatton's advice. Lewger shortly afterwards, with Hatton's assent, conveyed the manor of St. John's to Henry Fox for five thousand pounds of tobacco, half of which sum should be paid to Bennett. Randall[2] in an able address has pointed out that Bennett had quite probably come into Maryland with his wife as early as 1646. He was a member of the grand jury at St. Mary's in December, 1648.[3] On January 7, 1649/50, Durand applied for nine hundred acres of land for having transported into the Province himself and seven other persons in March, 1648/9. The first actual certificate for land in what became Anne Arundel County was issued to Richard Beard on January 6, 1650/1, for two hundred acres on the south side of South River. On March 17, 1650, George Puddington, one of the prominent Puritans, asked for a grant of eight hundred acres of land for "having transported into this Province, at his own expense the previous year, himself and 7 persons," and a number of similar applications follow on the land records.

News of the reception of the Puritans, of Baltimore's time-serving policy, possibly of his failure to have Charles

---
[1] 10 Md. Arch., Prov. Ct., 66, 70; Davis, 69.
[2] J. W. Randall, 11.
[3] 4 Md. Arch., Prov. Ct., 321, 447, 521.

II promptly proclaimed as his father's successor, reached that claimant of the English throne,[1] and from his place of exile on the Continent he issued a commission on February 16, 1649/50, to Sir William Davenant, the poet, Shakespeare's godson, constituting him Governor of Maryland, "alleging therein the reasons to be, because the Lord Baltimore did visibly adhere to the rebels in England and admitted all kinds of sectaries and Schismatics and ill affected persons, into that plantation." It is quite probable that this commission was sent from Breda, on June 20, 1650, when a commission was sent Berkeley as Governor of Virginia. The Queen Henrietta Maria is said to have sent out Davenant with weavers and mechanics, but his ship was captured and that danger averted from the Province.

In the spring of 1649 Stone had left Maryland for a short period, probably to go to Virginia, and on May 2 he appointed Greene[2] as his deputy, directing that Hatton, the Secretary, succeed in case of Greene's refusal. Stone had returned before July 7, and again left the Province in Greene's hands on September 20, 1649. After Stone had been absent for a few weeks, on November 15 Greene was guilty of the crass stupidity of proclaiming Charles II as King[3] and pronouncing a general pardon to all the inhabitants of the Province upon that occasion.[4] It is uncertain when Stone returned to Maryland, but he was back[5] before January 24, 1649/50. A day or two after the beheading of Charles I, the House of Commons by ordinance had declared that any person "who should presume to declare Charles Stuart, son of the late Charles," to be King, "should

---

[1] Bozman, II, 409, 675. D. R. Randall (A Puritan Colony, 25) thinks that Berkeley had reported to Charles II that Baltimore had given shelter to heretics. Neill, Founders of Maryland, 126; The Lord Baltimore's Case, concerning the Province of Maryland adjoining to Virginia in America; Langford, A Just and Cleere Refutation. For Davenant's commission see Maryland Historical Magazine, I, 21.
[2] 3 Md. Arch., Coun., 231.
[3] 4 Md. Arch., Prov. Ct., 496; 3 Md. Arch., Coun., 242; Bozman, II, 377.
[4] 3 Md. Arch., Coun., 243.
[5] 4 Md. Arch., Prov. Ct., 538; 1 Md. Arch., Ass., 259.

be deemed and adjudged a traitor." Scotland, Ireland, and Virginia supported the royal cause for a time; but, though news of Charles's death must have come to Maryland months before Greene's proclamation, Stone had followed Cecilius Calvert's cautious policy and had taken no action. Maryland was peculiarly fortunate in not being required to announce her position, as writs in the Province ran in the name of the Proprietary, not in that of the King, and Greene's act was of a most foolhardy character, besides being unsuitable from a mere locum tenens.

When Greene took the oath as Governor that September,[1] he did not do so without reservation, as he should have done, and when seated in office he resolved to act contrary to Hatton's advice. Hatton, fearing that Greene's conduct, probably in proclaiming Charles II as King, "might much prejudice" Baltimore, showed Greene, at a Council meeting, another deputation of the office of Governor from Stone to the Secretary, upon the production of which the deputation of Greene became void. Hatton later wrote the Proprietary[2] that Greene still pressed on to accomplish his plans and furthermore said, insolently, "Although Baltimore should send directions to the contrary, I would do the same." Baltimore answered Hatton's letter by writing Stone, on August 6, 1650, that all things done by Greene as Governor are to be null and void, excepting such of them as Stone shall confirm. But the mischief had been done and Baltimore's enemies had been given their opportunity. Hatton did not get along well with the Roman Catholics, and one Walter Pakes complained to Baltimore about certain speeches of the Secretary with reference to those of that religion.[3] Hatton, by his own oath and by the testimony of the Assembly of 1650, however, fully cleared himself, in Baltimore's eyes, of "that foul imputation."

We must never forget that the Lord Proprietary was a great landowner as well as a ruler, and his anxiety to secure

---
[1] 1 Md. Arch., Ass., 313.
[2] We assume this from Baltimore's letter to Stone of August 6, 1650.
[3] 1 Md. Arch., Ass., 318; Davis, 247.

settlers on his land and rents from them explains many of his actions. His Governors were also his land agents, and in carrying out this agency, Stone, on April 13, 1649, issued a proclamation[1] commanding all "adventurers or planters" in the Province to take grants for their lands from the Proprietary, that the lapse of time might not make their rights doubtful and deprive Baltimore of his rents. From February, 1644, when the Provincial great seal was violently taken away, until the recent arrival of a new seal no one could receive a legal grant, but now the seal had come, and all persons resident in Maryland or Virginia who "pretend any right" to lands in the Province, as due them by the Conditions of Plantation, or by any other warrant from Baltimore given prior to March 17, 1648/49, but who had not yet received patents, were ordered to prove their right to the Governor before November 1. Persons absent from either Maryland or Virginia might have until March 25, 1650, to obtain grants, and if any failed to prove their right within the specified time, they "must blame their own obstinacy, if hereafter they be refused any such grants." On October 30 Greene, who was acting Governor, issued a second proclamation extending the time for all persons until March 25, as divers who had land could not have it surveyed in the time formerly limited without great damage by leaving their crops.[2] On March 25, 1650, Stone issued a third proclamation stating that certain persons had not acted under the former proclamations on pretence of not having notice of them, and, to the end that no man might justly pretend ignorance,[3] he extended the period further until Michaelmas (September 29). The most interesting result of this proclamation is that the Jesuits filed application on

---

[1] 3 Md. Arch., Coun., 229; Bozman, II, 374. Bruce in his Economic History of Virginia in the Seventeenth Century, I, 139, says that Bullock (Virginia, 4) is authority for the statement that some Virginians were in the habit of retiring into Maryland as soon as the heats of summer arrived, and that there they enjoyed uninterrupted good health.
[2] 3 Md. Arch., Coun., 243.
[3] 3 Md. Arch., Coun., 253.

Provincial Conditions in 1649–50. 15

August 14, 1650, for land due them for transporting fourteen men and a woman in 1633 and five men in 1634.[1] There was still difficulty in the collection of rents, and on January 8, 1650/1, Stone, by proclamation, directed all the people of St. Mary's County to pay their rents to the Secretary before February 12 next.[2] No rigorous course was taken then, however, and on December 2, 1651, Stone a second time warned[3] the people of St. Mary's County and all others whose rents were payable at St. Mary's to pay Hatton before January 10 under penalty. Still there were arrears of rent left unpaid, and on March 20, 1651/2, Stone issued another proclamation stating that he would have the sheriff distrain upon the property of any inhabitant of the Province owing rent and not paying it within a fortnight.[4]

Bozman calls attention to the fact that no grants of lands to the Puritans whom Stone induced to come into Maryland are to be found prior to the creation of their settlement into Anne Arundel County in 1650, and remarks that the proclamations, to which we have referred, "strongly indicate the general opinion, which appears to have been now quite prevalent, . . . of the precarious continuance of the Lord Proprietary's government over the Province." "Planters and adventurers, who had obtained warrants for tracts of land, probably flattered themselves, that by a little patience and neglect in taking out grants, they would speedily be relieved from any rents to be claimed by his lordship."

On July 2, 1649, Cecilius Calvert signed, at London, new Conditions of Plantation, which he sent to Stone to be published in the Province.[5] They state that the Conditions of 1648 seem not "to give sufficient encouragement to many to adventure or plant" in Maryland, and they provide that he who imports thirty persons may have a grant of a manor

---
[1] 3 Md. Arch., Coun., 258.
[2] 3 Md. Arch., Coun., 260.
[3] 3 Md. Arch., Coun., 267.
[4] 3 Md. Arch., Coun., 268.
[5] Bozman, II, 377; 3 Md. Arch., Coun., 231; Kilty, The Land-Holder's Assistant, and Land-Office Guide, 47.

16   Maryland Under the Commonwealth.

of three thousand acres, while formerly the limit was two thousand acres for the importation of twenty persons, and that for every person imported one hundred acres, instead of fifty, should be given on the payment of the same rent, namely, one shilling for each fifty acres. Bozman notes that the place of signature shows that Baltimore was not in particular ill favor with the Commonwealth.

A few months later Richard Ingle's hostility toward Baltimore was shown in a petition and remonstrance sent to the Council of State, which was read[1] on November 14, 1649, and referred to the consideration of the Committee for the Admiralty. The Council appointed December 20 for taking into consideration the business of Virginia and Maryland, but deferred the matter for a week, after hearing Ingle and Robert Rawlins, and summoned Baltimore and a number of merchants, among whom was Thompson, Claiborne's former partner. The matters were deferred to January 10, 1649/50, and again, after seven more postponements, to March 4. On February 19 Ingle complained concerning two ships going to Virginia. This remonstrance also was referred to the Committee for the Admiralty, who had power to stay the ships if they saw cause. Finally, on March 15, we discover that Ingle's complaint referred to the old commission from Charles I to Leonard Calvert in 1643, authorizing him to seize Parliamentary ships. The Committee directed the Attorney General and another lawyer to consider the "validity and invalidity of the original grant" of Maryland in 1632. Then came more delay and additional postponement, until October 3, when a petition was presented to the Council "on behalf of divers well affected persons of the Isle of Providence in Maryland."[2] As Parliament was considering the validity of the patents of the colonies, the Council referred the matter to a committee of their own number.

---

[1] 3 Md. Arch., Coun., 244-250, 252, 253. See "A Declaration shewing the illegality and unlawfull proceedings of the Patent of Maryland, 1649," in Brodhead, Documents Relative to the Colonial History of the State of New York, III, 23. The Virginia Magazine of History and Biography, XVII, 21.
[2] 3 Md. Arch., Coun., 254, 259.

For nearly a year from this time Maryland drops from the English records, save[1] that Richard Thurston, commander of a ship, was given leave to go to Maryland with his vessel to collect some debts and to trade, "provided he trades not with any places in defection to this Commonwealth," and that William Mitchell, "with his company, their families, servants, goods and necessaries," was given a like pass on September 3. Finally, on December 23, 1651, the Council of State read Baltimore's petition,[2] and ordered that he "be left to pursue his cause according to law and that, as things concerning the same shall be offered at the Council, the Council will take notice thereof as there shall be occasion."

While in these doubtful circumstances a heavy blow fell on Baltimore, for on July 23, 1649, his wife, the Lady Anne Arundel, died, aged thirty-four years. He described her on her tomb at Tisbury as "pulcherrima et optima conjux."[3]

II. THE ASSEMBLY OF 1650.

On January 24, 1649/50, Governor Stone issued a proclamation for the election of burgesses to an Assembly to be held at St. Mary's on the second of the next April.[4] The writ recited that "the manner of summoning Assemblies . . . is wholly left to the Lord Proprietor's discretion,"[5] and it directed all freemen of St. Mary's County to appear in person or by proxy, each freeman being limited to two proxies. An alternative method, which was actually used, was that the freemen of each hundred choose burgesses. If the freemen of each hundred did not agree as to whether they would be represented by proxies or by burgesses, they must all appear personally. The original writ assigned one

---
[1] 3 Md. Arch., Coun., 263.
[2] 3 Md. Arch., Coun., 267.
[3] Neill, Terra Mariae, 88. In the Historical Magazine, 2nd Series, III, 176, W. Willis speaks of a medal struck in her honor.
[4] 1 Md. Arch., Ass., 259.
[5] See 1 Md. Arch., Ass., 266; "Maryland Notes, 1650," by H. H. Goldsborough, William and Mary College Quarterly, V, 47, 131; Davis, 71.

burgess to St. Clement's and St. Mary's, one or two to St. George's, St. Inigoes, and St. Michael's, and two or three to Newtown Hundred; but the freemen of St. Mary's earnestly requested[1] that they might have two burgesses, as they were "the ancientest hundred and the first seated within this Province under his Lordship's government," and their petition was granted. Newtown, St. Michael's, and St. George's took advantage of the largest number allowed, but St. Inigoes sent only one burgess, so that eleven men represented St. Mary's County. To the Isle of Kent County a writ was sent for the election of one, two, or three burgesses, and Robert Vaughan, the sheriff, returned himself elected as the sole burgess.[2] When April 2 came, however, only the St. Mary's men appeared, and for a few days Stone adjourned the Assembly, which now met in two houses,[3] while he went in person to "that part of the Province now called Providence" and presided on Friday, April 5, at the choice of two burgesses by that Puritan settlement. On his return with those burgesses on the following day, Stone found that Vaughan had arrived, and the Assembly organized by the election on the part of the Lower House of James Coxe, one of the Puritans, as Speaker, and William Bretton as Clerk.[4]

The ascendancy of Protestants in this Assembly is noteworthy, and shows that there was no good ground for the accusation that the Proprietary unduly favored the members

---

[1] 1 Md. Arch., Ass., 260.
[2] Vaughan was also a Councilor but sat in either house, 1 Md. Arch., Ass., 261, 285.
[3] In 1649 the formula at the foot of each law was: "The freemen have assented. Enacted by the Governor." In 1650 the latter sentence remains the same, the former one is divided and reads: "The Lower House hath assented. The Upper House hath assented," 1 Md. Arch., Ass., 250, 286.
[4] The record says April 6, Sabbath (i. e., Saturday), 1 Md. Arch., Ass., 261. Stone, Hatton, Price, and Vaughan were Protestants, Greene was a Roman Catholic, Pile's religion is uncertain, and it is not known that he was present. Of the burgesses Coxe and Puddington of Providence, Vaughan, Sherman, Hatch, Beane, Brough, Robins, and Posey were Protestants, while Land, Brooke, Matthews, Manners, and Medley were Roman Catholics. Fenwick, a Protestant, later replaced Matthews, see Johnson, "The Foundation of Maryland," Maryland Historical Society, Fund Publication no. 18, and Davis, 207.

The Assembly of 1650.

of his own faith. The Governor and at least three of the five Councilors and nine of the fourteen burgesses were Protestants, and a new election made the membership of the Lower House stand 10 to 4. There was "foul weather" on the sixth, so that three of the burgesses could not come.[1] The other eleven took a burgess's oath drawn up by Hatton for Stone at the burgesses' request, pledging the members to faithful performance of duty, to endeavors for advanceing "the Lord Proprietor's just rights and privileges and the public good of this Province," and to secrecy as to what might pass in the Assembly.[2] A Clerk's oath was also prepared, and all those present took the oaths. On Monday, April 8, came the three burgesses who had been absent on Saturday. Two of them promptly took the oath; the third, Thomas Matthews, of St. Inigoes Hundred, refused and was given until afternoon to consider the matter. In the afternoon he continued in his refusal, stating that he could not take the oath and have free exercise of his religion, as the obligation to secrecy prevented him from telling his father confessor of what occurred in the house and so from being "guided in matters of conscience by his spiritual counsel."[3] Matthews was promptly "expelled and discharged of his place and vote," a new election in the hundred was ordered on the eleventh, and Cuthbert Fenwick was elected in Matthews's room. He appeared on the eighteenth and agreed to take the oath, "provided that it might not prejudice in any sort his religion or conscience." The House voted that he must take the oath "without any reservation," but might consider the matter till the morrow. In the afternoon, however, the House declared that the oath of secrecy was not meant to infringe liberty of conscience or religion, and Fenwick was thereupon sworn. Greene, however, the Roman Catholic member of the Council, had uttered "harsh speeches,"[4] taxing the House with injustice in expelling

---
[1] Hatch, Beane, and Matthews, 1 Md. Arch., Ass., 274.
[2] 1 Md. Arch., Ass., 261; Bozman, II, 383.
[3] 1 Md. Arch., Ass., 274–278.
[4] 1 Md. Arch., Ass., 276, 277.

Matthews, so on the tenth the Lower House sent a petition to the Upper House by their Speaker, "desiring vindication." In the debate upon the petition the Lower House felt that it was wrong for their members to take the oath of secrecy when the Upper House did not do the same, and it voted to petition the Upper House that members of the Council refusing to take the same oath should not have vote or seat in the Upper House during the Assembly.[1] No answer to the petition was made until the eighteenth, when the burgesses asked for a reply and were informed that the power of the Lower House to expel a member, when the Governor was not present, is denied, but that Matthews "expelled himself," as he did not come to "demand his voice, after the Governor himself was present in the House."[2] The Upper House must have taken the oath of secrecy, however, for on Monday, April 29, when the Assembly adjourned, both houses declared that no further secrecy was required after the close of the session.[3]

On the first day of the session order was given for "drawing the act and orders for settling the house,"[4] and these documents, probably drafted by Hatton, were submitted, and being unanimously adopted, were signed by Stone. The act for settling the Assembly formally adopted the bicameral system, and his division into two houses remained in force during the whole time of the Proprietary government.[5] The Upper House should consist of Stone and Hatton, with any one or more of the Council, while the lower one was composed of the fourteen burgesses, of which number five should be a quorum. Henceforth bills must be passed by the major part of both houses before the Governor signed them. The rules of order for the two houses were the same and were similar to those of previous legislatures, the only new features of importance being that the tobacco which

---

[1] Bozman (II, 388) gives this explanation of this troublesome matter.
[2] This restraint upon the Lower House is noteworthy.
[3] 1 Md. Arch., Ass., 284; Bozman, II, 390.
[4] April 2, 1 Md. Arch., Ass., 261.
[5] 1 Md. Arch., Ass., 273; Bozman, II, 385.

should accrue from fines on the burgesses was directed to be disposed of toward the relief of the poor.

On Saturday, April 6, the Conditions of Plantation were read,[1] as well as a long letter written to Stone and the General Assembly by Baltimore from London on August 26, 1649. The Proprietary is aggrieved that the sixteen laws were not passed. Stone, it seems, by a letter to Baltimore of the preceding twentieth of February had acknowledged the receipt of the code of laws and stated that "they were so just and reasonable, as that upon due consideration they ought to be well liked of by well affected men," yet the Assembly refused to enact all of them. This failure, the Proprietary hears, was caused "by the subtile suggestions of some, who ought rather to have assisted in promoting . . . a good correspondence, rather than to raise . . . jealousies or discontents." The report to Baltimore had been that the act of recognition of the charter and that for the oath of fidelity were the chief stumbling-blocks, as they contained the words "Absolute Lord and Proprietary" (which Baltimore reminds them is the exact title given in the charter) and "Royal Jurisdiction." Some said that the former term infers a slavery in the people of Maryland and the latter one exceeds the charter powers; Baltimore denies that the "former words import . . . such odious and sinister interpretation," or that he has any intention to enslave the people. The acts themselves prove this, having provision for freedom of conscience, for freedom from taxes except those laid with the Assembly's consent, for freedom from martial law except "in time of camp, or garrison, and within such limits," for freedom of trade with the Indians, on conditions tending more to the public good than to Baltimore's advantage. The charter gives Baltimore all the jurisdiction which the Bishops of Durham ever possessed, and "such as are best read in antiquities" know that prior to the reign of Henry VIII the Bishop had royal jurisdiction.[2] Bozman acutely remarks that the objection to the Proprietary's royal

---

[1] 1 Md. Arch., Ass., 262; Bozman, II, 367.
[2] Bozman, II, 368.

jurisdiction ran deeper than Baltimore supposed, and was not so much based on the supposition that his assumption of it was contrary to the charter, but rather "emanated from the same Republican spirit, which had destroyed the monarchy in England and now, diffusing itself into the minds" of the Puritans in Maryland, "began to exercise its animosities against everything that looked like monarchy under a colonial government."[1] Baltimore's letter shows clearly that he thinks that the Jesuits are at the bottom of the movement to reject his laws,[2] they hoping, in the division and faction which may follow, to revive their claim to lands given by or bought from the Indians for them. The Proprietary knows that his right to the Province needs no confirmation by the Assembly, but is derived from his charter and his "dear purchase" by the "expense of great sums of money, with much solicitude and travail;" yet he wonders that any well-affected person should be "backward in concurring to a public act of recognition." He urges the legislature to accept the whole sixteen laws as "more necessary for the people's good and the public there than for our own interests." In strong words Baltimore insists upon the legality of the Assembly of 1646/7, protests against the remonstrance of the Assembly of March, 1647, and disassents to several acts passed at that session.

In answer to the letter sent him by the Assembly of 1649 the Proprietary states that he also desires a good understanding with the people of the Province, but must repudiate the disposition of his cattle to Leonard Calvert for the payment of the soldiers who recovered the Province for Baltimore. With surprising pettiness Baltimore seems to have expected this payment to be borne by the Province, and states that only Lewger had the power to dispose of the Proprietary's personal estate, and Lewger denies that he joined in any such grant. Baltimore feels that the injustice shown him is aggravated by the rejection of the payment of the customs

---
[1] Strong, Babylon's Fall.
[2] 1 Md. Arch., Ass., 264.

The Assembly of 1650. 23

due him by act of January, 1646/7, for better enabling him to defend the Province, which grant of customs was doubtless a powerful reason for his upholding the validity of the Assembly which granted it. If Leonard Calvert disposed of his brother's personal estate, he must have done so in confidence of gaining a return from these customs, but after his death the customs grant was taken away. The Assembly of 1649 had expressed the wonder that Baltimore should deprive of their just dues those who had done good service in the recovery of the Province, and he now replies that in the sixteen laws he had especially provided that such persons be paid by an equal assessment on all the inhabitants, "which is the justest and usual way in all civil kingdoms and commonwealths for defraying of public charges." The prince of a state should not bear the charge of a war from his own private fortunes, and in all countries, when a tax is laid and soldiers or officers have an estate, they pay their proportionable part of the tax. Baltimore is certain that many in Maryland have deserved well of him and he will not be unmindful of them, but he states that men have often by some actions deserved very well of others, but afterwards by other actions have "quite drowned the merit" of the former ones. In case the sixteen laws are passed and sixteen cows and a bull are delivered to the commissioners of the treasury for Baltimore's use[1] according to the Act of 1649, the Proprietary states that he will allow half of the customs due him for tobacco laden on any Dutch ship toward the satisfying of just claims touching the recovery of the Province. William Thomson, the only Roman Catholic who took Ingle's oath against Baltimore, and who gave a third of his cattle to the rebels, is forgiven, as the Assembly had asked. Stone is directed to investigate whether Abraham Janson, a Dutchman, had exported tobacco without paying duty. Cattle without known owners must be delivered to Baltimore's agents, as they come under his right to waifs and strays. With pious expressions of hope

[1] 1 Md. Arch., Ass., 252.

for future unity and prosperity of the Province, the letter closes.

After the letter was read and the Assembly was organized, the burgesses asked leave to debate and advise concerning the sixteen laws, and as this consultation would require a long time, the Governor adjourned the Upper House until Wednesday, April 10.[1] On Monday, April 8, after expelling Matthews, the Lower House read the sixteen laws, and on Tuesday the act of recognition and the act of oblivion were discussed.[2] There was evidently some objection to the former law, and the Speaker ordered that an act should be drawn up for the rights of the Lord Proprietor and the people's liberties. On Wednesday the Lower House presented to the upper one a report, now lost, upon the sixteen laws, with their petition before referred to.

On Thursday Mr. Robert Clarke[3] was added to the Upper House, and there was some discussion as to whether the act of recognition could not be passed as a temporary law with right to repeal, if it infringed men's liberties or consciences. A joint committee of the two houses was then appointed for perusal of the sixteen laws, that there might be "more speedy dispatch." The committee consisted of two Councilors and six burgesses,[4] and while it met the Assembly adjourned. On Wednesday, April 17, the "Committee delivered in their certificate," which is now lost, and which was sent to the Lower House. On the same day a remarkable document was prepared.[5] It is not entered in the Provincial records and is known only because copied in Langford's "Refutation of Babylon's Fall," a pamphlet of which we shall speak later. The document is signed by Stone,

---

[1] 1 Md. Arch., Ass., 274.
[2] 1 Md. Arch., Ass., 275.
[3] 1 Md. Arch., Ass., 276. The Governor remitted all the fines of the Assembly. Clarke was put on the Committee of Laws. On April 20 at his own request he was discharged from sitting further, 1 Md. Arch., Ass., 279.
[4] Vaughan ranked as a burgess. The Councilors were one Protestant and one Roman Catholic and the burgesses five Protestants and one Roman Catholic.
[5] Davis, 71.

Price, Vaughan, and Hatton[1] of the Council, eight Protestant burgesses and forty-three other Protestants, which last number is headed by the name of William Durand and includes residents both of St. Mary's and of Providence.[2] The pith of the declaration is a statement "to all persons whom it may concern, that, according to an act of assembly here, and several strict injunctions and declarations by his ... lordship ..., we do here enjoy all fitting and convenient freedom and liberty in the exercise of our religion under his lordship's government; and that none of us are in any ways troubled or molested, for or by reason thereof."

On the eighteenth the committee's report was referred back to it,[3] to see if they wished to make alteration or addition, and on Friday the nineteenth the report was again discussed by the Lower House, which decided not to accept the act requiring that all persons accounting do so under oath, but rather to draw up a new act imposing a penalty upon false accounts.[4] The law as drawn up by the Lower House was assented to by the upper one, and finally met with Baltimore's approval, as it required those entrusted with personal property for the use of the Proprietary to account for it under oath, while the oath was not required of others making account.

In addition to the sixteen laws, certain other bills, orders, and petitions were before the Assembly, and on Monday, April 22, Stone appointed the Speaker, Vaughan, and four other burgesses[5] as a committee to examine these matters and report on Wednesday. The committee, under Fenwick's chairmanship, met with two of the Councilors[6] on Tuesday and Wednesday and discussed a number of bills, some of which were afterwards enacted, while others were not. On Wednesday afternoon the committee re-

---
[1] Thomas Greene was away, 1 Md. Arch., Ass., 277.
[2] Bozman, II, 672. Neither Fuller's nor Bennett's name is there.
[3] 1 Md. Arch., Ass., 278.
[4] 1 Md. Arch., Ass., 279, 306.
[5] 1 Md. Arch., Ass., 279; two Roman Catholics and two Protestants.
[6] 1 Md. Arch., Ass., 280; Greene and Price.

ported to a joint session of the two houses, and Hatton was directed to write to Baltimore informing him as to what was done with regard to his sixteen laws. This letter was read before a joint session of the two houses of the Assembly on the next day, and was signed by the Governor, three Councilors, and all the burgesses except four, all of whom were Roman Catholics and one of whom was probably absent.[1] On the same day Stone appointed two Councilors and six burgesses, of whom one was the only Roman Catholic who signed the letter and two others were the representatives of Providence, to review the laws of 1649, especially that one concerning the provision of cattle for Baltimore, and any other acts and orders, drawn but not read.[2] Captain John Price was chairman of the committee, which met on Friday, and besides considering several proposed acts, reported that all the laws of 1649 should be continued, except that the prohibition of the export from the Province of cattle formerly belonging to the Proprietary should be continued for another year.[3] The members were becoming weary of the session and hastened through the consideration of the committee's report[4] on Saturday and Monday, adopting in joint session of the two houses most of the recommendations, though one act, "providing punishment for capital offenses," was ordered to be set aside till next Assembly, as there was a tie vote in the Lower House upon it.[5]

When the adjournment of the session was discussed, some one said that those attending the Assembly ought to be protected from arrest, but the burgesses replied that they desired no protection, and preferred to be liable to all suits.[6] The Governor finally prorogued the legislature to January 10, 1651.

---

[1] Greene did not sign. Possibly two were absent, as John Medley, who did not sign, was permitted on that day to go home on account of his wife's illness.
[2] 1 Md. Arch., Ass., 281. John Halfhead's petition was referred to the Provincial Court, as neither party was present.
[3] 1 Md. Arch., Ass., 295, 253. The three enactments considered in this statute were called orders, not acts, in 1649.
[4] 1 Md. Arch., Ass., 282, 285. Fenwick alone opposed this speed.
[5] 1 Md. Arch., Ass., 283.
[6] 1 Md. Arch., Ass., 284.

The Assembly of 1650.

Before adjournment the Committee on Laws also brought[1] in "the Country's charges" and those of the burgesses to be laid on each county or hundred particularly for its own representatives. As they could not make a true estimate of the population in the several counties, the levy of the assessment was postponed until October,[2] when Stone should summon three or four of the Puritans, one or two from Kent and one or two out of each hundred in St. Mary's. These deputies, chosen by the freemen of these counties and hundreds, should assemble on October 10 at St. Mary's under the Governor's presidency[3] and make assessment of the levy on the taxable persons per poll. The Governor was allowed six men and each Councilor three men free of taxes. These men must be the "own proper servants" or live in the house of the officer who claimed the exemption.[4]

The acts of this Assembly are of four classes: first, nine laws introduced by the Assembly and called acts; second, eleven laws, called orders, of a more temporary character; third, two confirmatory laws; and fourth, ten laws called acts, which are probably among the sixteen laws. In the first class are found the act for the organization of the Assembly, which we have already discussed; provisions for the punishment of adultery, fornication, false witness, swearing on secular days,[5] drunkenness, striking an officer of the law, or any one in the presence of a court; provisions for fixing the Secretary's and sheriff's fees[6] and the salary of the

---

[1] 1 Md. Arch., Ass., 282. William Lewis was allowed four hundred pounds of tobacco for bringing down the Indians last year. "Francis Brooke was not able through sickness to attend the house and drawing of his wine, the Committee think fit, not to provide for him at all," 1 Md. Arch., Ass., 284.
[2] 1 Md. Arch., Ass., 298.
[3] The Governor has a casting vote and must also assent to the determinations.
[4] 1 Md. Arch., Ass., 282.
[5] 1 Md. Arch., Ass., 286. Swearing on Sunday was forbidden by the act of 1649 concerning religion.
[6] 1 Md. Arch., Ass., 289. The sheriff's fees are continued as established by the Act of January, 1646/7; but I am inclined to think that the Assembly rather meant in making such confirmation to imply that Baltimore was wrong as to the legality of that Assembly session. In a later act of this session the fees are changed, p. 308.

muster master general.[1] In the same class is found "an act prohibiting all compliance with Capt. Wm. Claiborne in opposition to His Lordship's right and dominion over this Province."[2] The act recites the Privy Council proceedings of April 4, 1638, which confirmed Baltimore's title, and states that Claiborne now renews his claim in threatening letters to Stone, and "gives out in speeches that he purposeth ere long to make some attempt upon the Isle of Kent." Matters were in uncertain condition in England since the King's death, and Baltimore's arch-enemy would fish in the troubled waters. To prevent the success of his plans and to keep all the inhabitants of Maryland in their due obedience, the Assembly enacted a law that any resident of the Province who should assist Claiborne or any of his adherents in any enterprise against the Island or any other place within the Province should be punished by death and confiscation of all his Maryland property, both real and personal, to the use of the Proprietary.

The disturbed conditions of affairs in Maryland and in England had resulted in the neglect for a long time of the seating of land by divers persons who had taken it up, and in the desertion of plantations by others who had once seated them. These plantations were waste and uninhabited, but the owners kept their titles on foot, so that other persons could not take up the land. This was inconvenient to the Commonwealth[3] and a great injury to the Proprietary in the loss of rents and otherwise. To prevent this difficulty, the Assembly decreed[4] that plantations deserted for four years, unless owned by orphans under sixteen years of age, or claimed with payment of rents in arrears before March 25, 1651, might be regranted by the Proprietary. For the future a similar regrant of deserted plantations might be made when the rent should be three years in arrears.

---

[1] 1 Md. Arch., Ass., 292.
[2] 1 Md. Arch., Ass., 287; Bozman, II, 391.
[3] Bozman (II, 392) properly draws attention to the use of this word instead of Province.
[4] Fenwick voted against this law, 1 Md. Arch., Ass., 282, 288. Bozman, II, 392.

The Assembly of 1650.   29

The Puritan immigration caused the Assembly to erect[1] that "part of the Province over against the Isle of Kent, formerly called Providence by the inhabitants, into a shire or county, by the name of Anne Arundel," the Lord Proprietary's wife, who had died in 1649. Other counties were laid out by the Proprietary in virtue of his Palatine jurisdiction. This is the only one formed before that loss of Baltimore's jurisdiction over the Province following upon the Revolution of 1689 which owes its existence to an act of the Assembly.

Another of these acts, caused by the murder by Indians, in a most barbarous and cruel manner, of two of the inhabitants of Kent and Anne Arundel Counties, prohibited any Indian from coming into these counties except to speak with the commander of the county upon some urgent occasion, when he was to give some known sign of his approach.[2] If this were done by the Indian, the inhabitants who met him must conduct him harmless to the commander. Any Indian coming otherwise might lawfully be killed by any inhabitant, and no one was allowed to harbor any Indian contrary to the direction of this act, which was to remain in force until repealed by the Governor's proclamation. This act was not the only result of the death of the two white men. One of the orders[3] provided for a march against the Indian tribes whose members were guilty of the murder, unless the murderers should be given up to the Provincial government.

Thomas Allen at his death[4] had left two children who had in some way been captured by Indians, and the estate was not sufficient to ransom them and pay all the debts.

---

[1] 1 Md. Arch., Ass., 292; Bozman, II, 393. Note that no boundaries are given the county. Randall, D. R. (A Puritan Colony, 22) thinks that the Puritans had determined to "found an independent community free from trials and conflicts attendant upon participation in the General Government of the Province."
[2] 1 Md. Arch., Ass., 291. Not over four Indians may come together. Bozman, II, 394. As a result of this law, by proclamation dated April 29, 1650, Stone revoked all licenses to Indians and foreigners to kill deer, 3 Md. Arch., Coun., 255.
[3] 1 Md. Arch., Ass., 294; Bozman, II, 395.
[4] 1 Md. Arch., Ass., 297; Bozman, II, 396; 4 Md. Arch., Prov. Ct., 403, 496, 527, 540; 10 Md. Arch., Prov. Ct., 50.

But the public charge this year would probably be "very great and burthensome," so the Assembly, with petty meanness, ordered that the children should be bound out as servants until they should arrive at the age of twenty-one to any one approved of by the Provincial Court who would pay the cost of their redemption. At the expiration of the term of service each child must receive a cow and a cow calf, three barrels of corn, and necessary clothing. If any person approved by the Provincial Court would deal more "favorably and charitably" with the children, taking them bound for a shorter time, or letting them go free, he should be first preferred.

The other orders confirm orders of the Assembly of 1649; provide for the assessment of the levy; prohibit engrossing of goods or servants;[1] direct the recording of the marks of cattle and hogs before Michaelmas;[2] forbid foreigners, "either English or Indian," to hunt in the Province without special license, on pain of forfeiture of equipment and imprisonment; allow Stone half a bushel of corn from every taxable person within St. Mary's and Kent Counties and from every freeman in Anne Arundel;[3] forbid Mr. Cuthbert Fenwick from transporting from the Province a horse which he has bought, which Mr. Thomas Thornborough claims was given him by Leonard Calvert, until the next General Assembly determined to whom the horse belongs.[4] They direct that "all maimed, lame, or blind persons within St. Mary's County" who cannot "get their living by working" shall be maintained as the Governor and Council think fit by an equal assessment on such inhabitants of the county as "shall not make a free and willing contribution out of their charitable dispositions."[5]

Still another order deals with the "reedifying of the fort of St. Inigoes,"[6] lest accidents happen, "much to the in-

---
[1] 1 Md. Arch., Ass., 294.
[2] 1 Md. Arch., Ass., 295.
[3] 1 Md. Arch., Ass., 295; 3 Md. Arch., Coun., 261, 267. Stone issued proclamations for the payment of this tax.
[4] 1 Md. Arch., Ass., 223, 280, 296; 4 Md. Arch., Prov. Ct., 347.
[5] 1 Md. Arch., Ass., 296. This begins Maryland's poor laws.
[6] 1 Md. Arch., Ass., 293.

The Assembly of 1650.

dignity of the Lord Proprietary" and "abuse of the Inhabitants, through the insolency and pride of some ill-minded people trading or trafficking here, if no place of force be maintained . . . to command their ships." A salary is provided for the gunner and a tax of powder, shot, and "match" for the use of the fort is laid on each ship trading in the Province. All vessels without special license are commanded, "both at their coming in and at their departure hence," to "ride 2 whole tides before and within command of the said fort and take discharge thence." The Governor may press six men and a captain, with necessary victuals and ammunition for a garrison, during the time that shipping are riding at anchor in the Potomac or St. George's River, and defray the charge of this garrison "by an equal assessment on all the inhabitants of this Province." For the repairing of the fort in the next autumn every five inhabitants of the Province must "find and maintain one man."

The third class of enactments consists of two signed statements of those persons who were members of this Assembly and had also served in those of 1647 and 1649 as to their understanding of the meaning of two acts passed in those Assemblies, which interpretations are adopted by this Assembly as law.[1]

The fourth class of laws is most important, containing ten acts, all but one of which, fixing the sheriff's fees,[2] are pretty clearly among the sixteen laws sent over by Baltimore. We have already examined the one concerning accounting and seen that the Assembly dared to amend it. We shall see that they exercised like daring with others of the laws, the first of which is "an act of recognition of the lawful and undoubted right and title" of Baltimore as "absolute Lord and Proprietary." I must own that I cannot see why Calvert insisted upon this act, which gave him noth-

---
[1] I Md. Arch., Ass., 299. See p. 321, where on April 22 five members of the Assembly of 1647 complain in a letter to Baltimore of Greene's conduct at that Assembly.
[2] I Md. Arch., Ass., 308.

ing which he did not already derive from his charter.[1] The act is couched in most fulsome terms of gratitude and loyalty and, in view of subsequent events, of hypocrisy. The term "absolute Lord" is no longer a stumbling-block; the legislators pledge themselves to "maintain, uphold, and defend" Baltimore "for ever, until the last drop of our blood be spent," "in all the royal rights, jurisdictions, authorities, and preeminences" given him by the charter, so far as these do not "prejudice the just and lawful liberties, or privileges, of the free born subjects of the Kingdom of England."[2] The act also refers to the "unspeakable benefits we have received by your Lordship's vigilancy" and to the "inestimable blessings" which Baltimore "poured on this Province, in planting Christianity among a people that know not God."

The next of these acts is one of oblivion, which pardons any of those in rebellion between February 15, 1644/5, and August 5, 1646, except Richard Ingle and John Durford, mariners, and such Kentishmen as Leonard Calvert had not pardoned. All contracts concerning plundered goods or cattle, to which another than the true owner was a party, shall be void at law. To preserve peace, all upbraiding of one man by another for acts done during this rebellion is forbidden.[3]

The next act is one "against raising of money within the said Province without Consent of the Assembly,"[4] and the fact that we can place such a law among those drafted for the Proprietary and sent to America by him is surely a fine proof of his wisdom and discretion as a ruler. The act recites that "the strength of the Lord Proprietary of this Province doth consist in the love and affection of his people, on which he doth resolve to rely upon all occasions for his

---

[1] 1 Md. Arch., Ass., 299. Bozman (II, 398) thinks that the adulation of Baltimore in the act shows that it was drafted in the Province. I cannot agree with him in this opinion.
[2] The word "Kingdom," doubtless in the original draft of 1648, escaped the Assembly's attention.
[3] 1 Md. Arch., Ass., 301; Bozman, II, 406.
[4] 1 Md. Arch., Ass., 302; Bozman, II, 400.

The Assembly of 1650. 33

supplies," and, therefore, he decrees "that no subsidies, aid, customs, taxes, or impositions shall hereafter be laid" upon the freemen of Maryland, or upon their personal property, without the consent of the major part of the freemen, or their deputies, declared in a General Assembly. Bozman clearly points out that the attempt of certain lawyers, at the commencement of the American revolution, to claim that this act had reference to parliamentary taxation was a mistaken one. Neither Baltimore nor the Provincial Assembly could speak on this point. The act was sent over by the Proprietary " to conciliate the good will of his colonists and to give them assurances that he meant not, for the future, to exercise even the semblance of arbitrary power, especially in taxation."

The next of the sixteen laws[1] is one " concerning the levying of war within this province," and it was referred to in Baltimore's letter of 1649. It decrees that the freemen need not aid, against their wishes, in the prosecution of any war made by the Proprietary or his Governor outside the limits of Maryland, unless the consent of the General Assembly has been obtained. Further, it limits the exercise of martial law to the time of war and the precincts of camp or garrison, and decrees that the charges arising from defence of the Province from invasion or from domestic insurrection shall be defrayed by an equal assessment upon the persons and estates of the inhabitants of Maryland.[2]

This law is not unrelated to the one " concerning trade with the Indians."[3] In contrast to the early monopoly of the trade in "beaver and other commodities," this trade is now thrown open to "every inhabitant of this Province," who may not only trade within Maryland, but also may pass on any river to trade with Indians without the Province, and may export from Maryland, without especial leave from the Governor, any commodity bought from the Indians except

---
[1] 1 Md. Arch., Ass., 302; Bozman, II, 402.
[2] This is to prevent another controversy like that over Leonard Calvert's acts in 1646.
[3] Bozman, II, 397; 1 Md. Arch., Ass., 307.

corn, paying a tenth in weight or value of all beaver to the Proprietor as customs duty. No such trader, however, was allowed to sell arms or ammunition to the Indians; nor should traders give the Indians just cause of offence, "whereby the public peace or safety of this Province may be endangered by any war;" nor enhance the price of corn, to the prejudice of the people; nor "go forth upon any such trade too weak in strength," whereby the Indians may be "emboldened to destroy them, or do them mischief." To prevent these mischances, persons desiring to enter the Indian trade must take out licenses from the Governor, which licenses he may not deny if the applicant gives reasonable security that he will comply with the above mentioned provisoes. Persons who are not inhabitants of Maryland, yet trade with the Indians therein without license under the great seal, shall have all their goods confiscated.

Two other acts forbid any one without special warrant from Baltimore to buy any ordnance, ammunition, cattle, servants, or goods belonging to the Proprietary,[1] and direct that debts due the Proprietary be paid before any other debts.[2]

We have left for the last the "act for taking of an oath of fidelity to the Lord Proprietary."[3] A similar oath with the words "royal jurisdiction" had been used in 1643 and probably also in more recent years, but the oath had been reworded and sent out by Baltimore from Bath on June 20, 1648, with the sixteen laws. All persons residing within the Province, or having an estate therein and coming themselves to Maryland, must take the oath according to the law, on pain of banishment for the first refusal and of fine and imprisonment for a second refusal. Though the members of the legislature had accepted the words "absolute" and "royal" in the act of recognition, they reject them in the oath, and merely provide that the oath-taker swear to be

---

[1] 1 Md. Arch., Ass., 303.
[2] 1 Md. Arch., Ass., 304.
[3] 1 Md. Arch., Ass., 304, 320; 5 Md. Arch., Coun., 149; Bozman, II, 403. Cf. 3 Md. Arch., Coun., 145, 193, 196. The Lord Baltamore's printed Case Uncased and Answered, 25.

faithful to Calvert as "Lord Proprietary" and to maintain his jurisdiction. They also add a clause that their faithfulness shall not be "any ways understood to infringe, or prejudice, liberty of conscience in point of religion," and insert the words "just and lawful" before the word "right" in the promise to defend Baltimore's interests.[1] These variations weaken the force of the oath, yet they leave it largely as it came from Baltimore's hands, so that we find an Assembly composed largely of Protestants and containing prominent members from the Puritan settlement at Providence adopting a most adulatory act of recognition, containing the words "absolute lord" and "royal jurisdiction," and agreeing that those who would not take an oath of fealty to the Proprietary shall be banished from Maryland.[2] It accords with the general mildness of Maryland's government that we learn from a statement made in 1655 that "no person within the Province was ever yet banished or fined for refusal" of the oath, only no land was granted to any one who would not take it.[3]

The laws, as passed in 1649 and 1650, were sent to Baltimore with the Assembly's letter, and on August 6, 1650, Cecilius makes gracious reply.[4] He has selected eighteen of the laws of these sessions, adding two to the sixteen previously sent by him, and had them engrossed, signed by himself, and sealed with his great seal. These laws are to remain permanently without change, except such as may be made with Baltimore's personal consent. To other temporary laws the Governors of the Province may assent, to

---
[1] Bozman (II, 404) calls our attention to the fact that Leonard Strong in Babylon's Fall wilfully mixes the oath of fidelity and the officer's oath.
[2] Langford says that the Puritans knew of the necessity to take an oath before they came to Maryland.
[3] Langford, A Just and Cleere Refutation. The oath of Governor and Councilor was even more optional. Langford says that the Puritans made no objection to the oath till they were much refreshed in the Province, and Browne (George Calvert and Cecilius Calvert, Barons Baltimore of Baltimore, 139) remarks that their alleging scruples of conscience concerning this oath seems "over niceness, since no scruple apparently intervened to prevent their breaking it when taken." See also Hammond, Leah and Rachel.
[4] 1 Md. Arch., Ass., 321, 386.

continue in force for a limited time unless the Proprietary sooner declare his disassent, and any law, except these eighteen permanent ones and such others as may in the future be added to that class, may be repealed by the two houses of the General Assembly with the Governor's consent. Thus there was created something very like a written constitution for the Province, in addition to that furnished in the charter.

III. Proprietor and Colonists, 1650-1.

On the same day on which he approved the acts Cecilius sent a long letter[1] to Stone, complaining of Greene's conduct while acting as Governor in the preceding autumn and stating that the letter of the Assemblymen, dated April 22, shows that in 1647 Greene "preferred his own ends of lucre and gain before our honor or profit."[2] For these reasons Greene's acts as Governor are to be null and void, unless confirmed by Stone, and Greene himself is to be removed from being a member of the "Council of State, Commissioner of our Treasury," and from all his other offices. Greene had been further accused to Baltimore of having made use of his privilege as a Councilor to protect himself from paying his debts. To prevent such a scandal hereafter, Baltimore decreed that every officer may be proceeded against "for any debt, trespass, crime, or misdemeanor," as was the case in Virginia. Stone was empowered to appoint some fitting person as receiver in Greene's room, for the time being, and to name as Councilors two able persons, "who are lately come, or may perhaps shortly come" to Maryland, and who "may be fit to be of our Council of State." Stone's appointees were to hold office until the Proprietary should "confirm or discharge them," and they must take the Councilor's oath. Stone was also empowered to pardon any criminal except those exempted by Baltimore's declaration of August 26, 1649, provided

---
[1] 1 Md. Arch., Ass., 313.
[2] 1 Md. Arch., Ass., 321; see 221, 232, 238.

those pardoned took the oath of fidelity, as passed by the legislature of 1650. This amended oath the Proprietary accepts and permits to be taken by those desiring warrants for tracts of land.

Baltimore went on to reply to the address sent him by the Assembly in April. He accepted the offer of sixteen cows and a bull, and stated that this acceptance shows "how great a desire" he had to "comply with them in any thing we can, though with much prejudice to ourself."

John Jarboe had "behaved himself unmannerly and contemptuously" toward Stone, and Baltimore directed his lieutenant to "cause such punishment to be inflicted on him as his fault deserveth"[1] unless he both made "public acknowledgment of his fault in open court," craved Stone's pardon, and promised better conduct in the future.

John Metcalf and William Lewis had both asked to be made sheriff of St. Mary's County, and as both were good men, Stone might appoint either one to that office. The Proprietor suggested that the other one be made receiver general in Greene's stead, if he were fit for the office. Lewis knew the Indian tongue, and Baltimore considered him a suitable person to be appointed interpreter general, if the Assembly could be induced to make him a reasonable allowance for that office. Such an allowance Baltimore would esteem a "particular respect shewed" him.

In his desire to increase the population of Maryland, Baltimore appointed Robert Brooke[2] as a member of the "Privy Council of State within our said Province of Maryland" by commission dated September 20, 1649. This honor, as well as the position of justice of the peace, was conferred upon Brooke because he "doth, this next sum-

---

[1] In the past Jarboe had merited well of Cecilius and of his "dear brother deceased."

[2] 3 Md. Arch., Coun., 240; Bozman, II, 376. This commission shows that the laying out of counties was deemed a matter within the executive powers of the royal jurisdiction of the Count Palatine of the Province. Bozman (II, 377) thinks that Brooke was a Puritan, as is shown by the favor the Parliamentary Commissioners showed him in 1652.

mer's expedition, intend to transport himself, his family and a great number of other persons and good store of provision and ammunition" into Maryland[1] to "settle a considerable plantation." A further honor was the appointment of Brooke as commander of one whole county, to be "newly set out round about and next adjoining" his settlement, and to contain as many square miles as are usually allotted counties in Maryland and Virginia.[2] Within the county Brooke could appoint six Commissioners having the same powers as those of Kent, could hold court and hear any criminal cases not extending to life or member, as well as civil causes not exceeding £10 sterling in damages or demands. Furthermore, he could appoint the sheriff and other necessary officers for the execution of justice, should himself be commander of the county militia, and was given the right of fortifying places for defence.

Nine days later the Proprietary appointed,[3] as Privy Councilor and justice of the peace, William Eltonhead, whose career in the Province was to have so tragic an end, and on March 4, 1649/50, he added a third member to the Council in the person of William Mitchell of Chichester, in Sussex, who proved to be a man of most unsavory character.[4] Mitchell, like Brooke, planned in the next summer to transport himself and family and divers others, artificers, workmen, and "other very useful persons, in all to the number of 20 persons at the least," and, after his plantation was established, he promised to provide fresh supplies of men, "as occasion shall serve."[5]

---

[1] A list of the persons who came with Brooke is found in Davis, 74.
[2] 3 Md. Arch., Coun., 238. The grant was not to conflict with any existing county. This is an amusing provision, as no Maryland county at the time had boundaries. On the Brooke family see Thomas, Chronicles of Colonial Maryland, 302, and the article by Dr. Christopher Johnston in Maryland Historical Magazine, I, 66, 181, 284, 376.
[3] 3 Md. Arch., Coun., 242.
[4] 3 Md. Arch., Coun., 250.
[5] Mitchell arrived in Maryland prior to December 10 (10 Md. Arch., Prov. Ct., 68), but was not sworn in until January 8, 1650/1 (10 Md. Arch., Prov. Ct., 52).

Proprietor and Colonists, 1650–1. 39

Brooke arrived[1] in Maryland June 30, 1650, with wife, ten children, eight of whom were boys, twenty-one menservants and seven women-servants, forty persons in all. On July 22 Brooke and his two elder sons, probably the only ones of full age, took the oath of fidelity, and on the same day Brooke and Eltonhead took the oath of Councilors. Late in the autumn, on November 21, the Governor and Council issued a proclamation constituting a territory south of the Patuxent River into Charles County and appointed Brooke its commander. The county was shortlived, and the order for its establishment was revoked by the Governor's order on July 3, 1654.[2]

When Baltimore made his arrangements with Captain Mitchell, he gave him a special warrant,[3] dated January 18, 1649/50, for a manor of three thousand acres, with the provision that one hundred acres should be deducted for each person wanting to make the number of those whom he transported thirty. Mitchell did not leave England until the autumn of 1650, but news had already been transmitted to Baltimore before August, 1651, that a mistake had been made in appointing Mitchell a Councilor, to which appointment the Proprietary was induced by Mitchell's "ability of understanding." Cecilius hoped that he would have been "a good assistance . . . for the better conduct of our government . . . and that, according to his serious professions to us, he would have, not only by his advice but also by his example of life, conduced much to the advancement of that Province." These hopes were vain. He fomented divisions. After his wife died on the voyage from England, he carried on adulterous relations with women whom he brought to Maryland with him, and in public discourse he profanely said that he was of no religion.[4] He was therefore removed

---
[1] 3 Md. Arch., Coun., 256.
[2] 3 Md. Arch., Coun., 260; Bozman, II, 377. The name was probably taken from the Proprietary's heir.
[3] Bozman, II, 424; 1 Md. Arch., Ass., 333; Kilty, 79. For various land entries, assignments, caveats, warrants, etc., of this period see Kilty, 86, 87, 89, 211, 213, 215, 216.
[4] See 10 Md. Arch., Prov. Ct., 173.

from his Councilorship, and Stone was ordered not to permit him to act in that station should he come again to the Province, whence he had returned to England.

On April 4, 1650, Mitchell executed a paper[1] stating that although he sent two of his children and his servants to Maryland, he intended to remain in England for a time. He empowered four of his servants[2] to manage all of his men-servants and boys, except his children and his cook, to use his iron ware and other truck, except the household stuff, which together with the ordering of the women-servants was left in the control of Anne Boulton, a servant. Mitchell planned to take with him a daughter of one William Smith as a servant, and offered to transport Smith to Maryland and then send him back to England without cost, that he might " be an eye witness how your child is disposed of."[3] Mitchell also recommended that Smith bestow household stuff upon his daughter, which Mitchell agreed not to mix with his own. Smith agreed to this and came with Mitchell, bringing some household stuff with him. When he arrived in the Province, however, he found[4] that the scoundrel refused to allow him " competent maintenance " there, to " pay for his passage for England," or to give him back his goods. He was just sixty years old, " an aged man and not

---

[1] 10 Md. Arch., Prov. Ct., 44.
[2] 10 Md. Arch., Prov. Ct., 67. When Mitchell arrived in the Province in the early winter he found that Hatton had boarded some of the servants for a while and he objected to Hatton's charges. The parties appointed arbitrators, and the amount these found due was awarded by the court to Hatton. On December 26, 1650 (10 Md. Arch., Prov. Ct., 120, 145), Mitchell bought three steers and a number of hogs, in return for which he agreed to give Kadger, the seller, the use of one of his servants until Mitchell's next arrival from England into the Province, when he would give Kadger the choice of any three servants whom Mitchell should import, tradesmen excepted. If he imported none, Kadger might pick any three of Mitchell's servants then in Maryland. Mitchell tried to evade the fulfilment of this contract and brought no men from England, but on March 22, 1651/2, the court decreed specific performance of the contract by giving Kadger three of Mitchell's servants in the Province. Brooke also sued him for goods and clothing furnished his people, 10 Md. Arch., Prov. Ct., 250, 257.
[3] 10 Md. Arch., Prov. Ct., 49.
[4] 10 Md. Arch., Prov. Ct., 78.

Proprietor and Colonists, 1650-1. 41

able, by his labors, to maintain himself." That he should not "perish in these foreign parts" he sued Mitchell, in June, 1651. Mitchell, who had not sat in the court since February, was absent in England, and Fenwick, who represented him, obtained a postponement of the case until January, 1651/2. Then the case was further postponed, upon Fenwick's agreeing to furnish Smith with a bed, of which he was in "extreme want."[1] In April, 1652, Mitchell finally appeared[2] in answer to Smith's suit, and declared that Hatton knew that Smith had agreed to be his servant in Maryland. Hatton was away on that day, but upon his return on the morrow he declared, " I know nothing to Capt. Mitchell's advantage." Mitchell was absent, but the court, in just indignation, declared that Mitchell's appearance on the preceding day was sufficient, as this is a "Court of Equity as well as Law," and condemned him to pay all that was asked and the costs of the suit brought by this old man, " seduced from his country, wife, and children by the fair and false promises " of Mitchell.

At the time Smith brought the suit, Mrs. Susan Warren, alias Williams,[3] Smith's daughter, who was a widow, confessed that she was with child by Mitchell, and the court ordered Fenwick to provide for her.[4] A charge was also made that Mitchell had endeavored to procure an abortion,[5] and evidence was given that Mitchell and the woman had lived in adulterous relations in Maryland.[6] In August she gave birth to a dead child.[7]

In April, 1652, Mrs. Warren petitioned that she might be set free from her service to Mitchell, alleging that he had received money from her to pay her passage.[8] In June

---
[1] 10 Md. Arch., Prov. Ct., 36.
[2] 10 Md. Arch., Prov. Ct., 164, 178.
[3] 10 Md. Arch., Prov. Ct., 174.
[4] 10 Md. Arch., Prov. Ct., 80.
[5] 10 Md. Arch., Prov. Ct., 81, 176, 177.
[6] 10 Md. Arch., Prov. Ct., 149.
[7] 10 Md. Arch., Prov. Ct., 171, 177. Mitchell's wife came with him to Maryland also, dying on the voyage, and there were dark rumors that he had poisoned her, 10 Md. Arch., Prov. Ct., 175, 177, 183.
[8] 10 Md. Arch., Prov. Ct., 161, 170, 178, 185, 259.

she was freed, and Mitchell was ordered to pay all the costs of the suit and of her imprisonment while she awaited trial. There was "much juggling and baseness in the whole business," but the court was satisfied that she was no servant. On Mitchell's return to the Province, on April 10, 1652, in the presence of Rev. Mr. Wilkinson, an Anglican clergyman, Mitchell, in an informal way, took as his wife one Joan Toast, a woman as godless as himself.[1]

When all these things were alleged against[2] him in June, 1652, Mitchell was committed to the common jail, charged with atheism, adultery, murder, abortion, and fornication, and Hatton prosecuted the case as State's Attorney.[3] A jury was sworn and brought in an indictment against Mitchell. On the next day Mrs. Warren was brought in, and Hatton accused her of adultery and the use of profane expressions. She pleaded guilty, and was punished by being "whipped with 39 lashes upon her bare back." Mitchell asked for no further jury, but for a court trial, and was ordered to pay five thousand pounds of tobacco and cask, to give bond for good behavior, to marry or leave his pretended wife, and to pay costs.[4]

On November 23, 1652, Smith sued[5] Mitchell for certain goods shipped from England upon his account, which goods Mitchell denied to have been Smith's. The case was postponed until January, when several of Mitchell's servants testified that Smith had come as a servant and that any goods brought over were Mitchell's. The case was again postponed until April, when the court decided to refer the whole matter to the next Assembly, and we hear no more of it.[6]

---
[1] 10 Md. Arch., Prov. Ct., 173.
[2] 10 Md. Arch., Prov. Ct., 182.
[3] 10 Md. Arch., Prov. Ct., 182. Mitchell drew up a petition for a speedy trial, which he intended to send to the Assembly, had it gone on.
[4] 10 Md. Arch., Prov. Ct., 184. Part of the fine was remitted.
[5] 10 Md. Arch., Prov. Ct., 202, 225, 228, 229.
[6] 10 Md. Arch., Prov. Ct., 251. In open court Smith taxed Price, one of the Council, with having said that the case betwixt Smith and Mitchell should never have an end, and then he begged Price's

Proprietor and Colonists, 1650–1. 43

Mitchell, in March, 1652/3, sued Nicholas Gwyther, sheriff of St. Mary's County, for serving a writ of execution on his estate granted by one who had no right to grant it and before a former execution made out against his person was duly returned,[1] for administering an oath to the appraisers on the execution, which he had no power to do, and for taking Mitchell's waistcoat, which was not valued. The sheriff answered that he had served an execution, granted according to the usual manner by Lieutenant Richard Banks, one of the Council, and that he had taken the waistcoat, together with one of Mitchell's children, out of charity, as Mitchell had fled the Province. Gwyther had been at some charge for the child's clothes above the small value of the waistcoat. Four members of the Council found no cause to censure the sheriff, and held the complaint to be "troublesome, vexatious, and impertinent," but the Governor was not satisfied and "respited the business."

Still another instance of Mitchell's duplicity was seen in the case which Francis Brooke brought against him.[2] Mitchell hired in England for fixed wages one Anne Boulton to go with him as governess of his children, and then sold her as an indentured servant to Brooke for two cows, but refused to deliver her two trunks containing her goods, to account for her wages, or to pay for some cloth he had taken from her. Brooke married her and they brought suit in June, 1653. Mitchell was out of the Province and the case was postponed until his return. In May, 1654, the case was finally brought to trial, Mrs. Brooke having died in the meantime, and the court gave full redress to Brooke with the court charges. Mitchell succeeded in securing a postponement of the judgment by suing out a writ of error on March 20, 1655, but the judgment was finally satisfied in 1656.

---

pardon. In June (10 Md. Arch., Prov. Ct., 273) Mrs. Warren, as her father's representative, was allowed a claim against Mitchell's estate. On May 31 Smith had given her a power of attorney (10 Md. Arch., Prov. Ct., 303).

[1] 10 Md. Arch., Prov. Ct., 256.
[2] 10 Md. Arch., Prov. Ct., 215, 268, 378, 389, 438.

44   Maryland Under the Commonwealth.

Stone[1] was absent from Maryland between May 22 and June 25, 1650, but it is significant that he appointed Hatton and not Greene as his deputy. Hatton seems to have been in high favor.[2] In his letter to Stone of August 6, 1650, the Proprietary said that Hatton had not received proper remuneration, but had to neglect his private affairs for public business, and should therefore have two thousand pounds of tobacco and cask. If he is too busy as Secretary to act as Attorney General, Stone may appoint some one else to the latter office.[3] Hatton evidently wished to keep both offices, for on January 10, 1650/1, Stone directed that he receive an annual salary of one thousand pounds of tobacco and cask as Attorney General.

We noticed that the Assembly of 1650 constituted the new county of Anne Arundel out of the Puritan settlement of Providence. To organize this county,[4] Stone appointed, on July 30, 1650, Edward Lloyd as commander and the following Commissioners: James Homewood, Thomas Mears, George Puddington, Matthew Hawkins, James Merryman, and Henry Catlyn. Their civil jurisdiction as a county court was limited to £20 sterling. Stone, by separate proclamation dated the preceding day, authorized Lloyd to grant warrants for land to any adventurers according to the Conditions of Plantation. Both of these documents were issued at Providence,[5] whither Stone had come to organize the county, and his desire to do so, in person and on the spot, was doubtless responsible for the delay of three months in carrying out the act of the Assembly.

During the summer of 1650 several inhabitants of the

---

[1] 3 Md. Arch., Coun., 255. February 25, 1649/50. Stone had revoked the appointment of Richard Husbands, mariner, as Admiral of the Province, because of Husbands's gross miscarriages. It seems that on the previous day Husbands, while "somewhat in drink," had fallen into an altercation with the notorious John Dandy on his ship in the St. George's River, 3 Md. Arch., Coun., 249.
[2] 3 Md. Arch., Coun., 261.
[3] 1 Md. Arch., Ass., 319.
[4] 3 Md. Arch., Coun., 257; Bozman, II, 406.
[5] 3 Md. Arch., Coun., 257. On the same day Vaughan was given the same power for Kent, 3 Md. Arch., Coun., 256.

Province obtained warrants from Stone to employ Indians to kill deer with guns, under color of which warrants the St. Mary's County people became "very much pestered with great concourse of Indians of several nations, to the annoyance and terror of divers of the inhabitants there and excessive waste and destruction of the game of this Province and dispersing and scattering of the cattle and hogs of the inhabitants, to their great prejudice and detriment."[1] To prevent a continuance of this state of things, Stone revoked all his warrants by proclamation of November 20, 1650, and directed all who had delivered any guns to any Indians to take them back.[2]

In November the Governor by advice of the Council permitted[3] a shipmaster to carry to the Mattapany Indians, "who were gone to seat towards the head of Patuxent River," some of their corn which he had on board his vessel.

In the same month a petition signed by sixteen men and a woman[4] was sent from Kent, complaining that, since the troublous times some five years ago, cattle had run wild on the island, and therefore the people were losing the increase of their herds and their tame cattle were carried away and spoiled by wild bulls. They therefore asked that the wild cattle be rounded up and disposed of. Mrs. Margaret Brent came to court and claimed that she and her brother were interested in this matter, as many of the cattle were theirs. The Provincial Court directed her and any other claimants to prove their right in the Kent County court. The county

---

[1] 3 Md. Arch., Coun., 260; 10 Md. Arch., Prov. Ct., 52. On January 8, 1650/1, two guns were brought into court, taken from two Indians employed by two settlers "without warrant as was alleged."
[2] Doubtless, as Henry Stockbridge wrote ("The Archives of Maryland as Illustrating the Spirit of the Times of the Early Colonists," Maryland Historical Society, Fund Publication no. 22, p. 47), "The cattle of the colonists, unrestrained, drew no nice distinctions between the crops of their owners and those of the Indians, and their hogs running at large seem to have been a novel and attractive species of game for the Indians, who could not understand why they should not protect their own crops, and hunt all animals running in the woods, as for generations they had been accustomed to do."
[3] 10 Md. Arch., Prov. Ct., 45.
[4] 10 Md. Arch., Prov. Ct., 48.

court should certify its finding to the Provincial Court, which would distribute the cattle as it saw fit, unless the claimants could agree to a distribution among themselves. Care must be taken to guard Baltimore's interests. Calvert on April 19, 1647, had directed two of the Kentishmen to take into their custody all neat cattle on the island belonging to absent persons.[1]

On January 31, 1651/2, Stone issued a writ to the sheriff of St. Mary's stating that information had come that Mrs. Mary Brent had recently caused to be killed "divers unmarked bulls and other cattle" on the Isle of Kent without lawful warrant, to which cattle Baltimore had a claim.[2] Some of the meat had been brought to St. Mary's for sale and must be secured until Mrs. Brent should show her right to it.

On March 25 the Provincial Court met and depositions were read that five wild unmarked bulls and four marked ones, two of which may not have been hers, were killed by her[3] orders in the preceding June, and that four casks of salted beef, which now needed repacking to prevent it from spoiling, were transported across the Bay. Hatton, as Attorney General, conducted the case for the Proprietary, and stated that as Mrs. Brent's agent had refused to repack it, Hatton had superintended the task and sold some of the meat to the best advantage he could. Mrs. Brent came to defend her own cause, and claimed that all the cattle killed were of her brother's own stock. She asked a jury trial, but the "Governor and Council being taken off upon other public urgent occasions could not attend the further hearing of the cause," and respited it, directing Hatton to sell the rest of the meat and be accountable therefor. By the time the next court met in April, Captain Claiborne,[4] "a man

---
[1] 10 Md. Arch., Prov. Ct., 60.
[2] 10 Md. Arch., Prov. Ct., 149.
[3] A little while before she had killed one unmarked wild bull. She was stated to have said that "she had a desire to kill all the unmarked bulls upon the island, if that she could," 10 Md. Arch., Prov. Ct., 348.
[4] 10 Md. Arch., Prov. Ct., 164, see 186.

Proprietor and Colonists, 1650-1.

now in power here," had made claim that he had some interest in the Kentish wild cattle, and that "the business did concern the whole Commonwealth" and so was more proper for an Assembly, to which body it was accordingly referred, and we hear no more of it.

To the three Councilors he named in 1650 Baltimore added two more in 1651. The first, Major-General Edward Gibbons,[1] of New England, a man of "honor, worth, and abilities," was commissioned Councilor, justice of the peace, and admiral of the Province on January 20, 1650/1. Gibbons had come to New England with Wollaston's company in 1625, and had remained behind when they were driven out. He united himself with the Puritans of Salem in 1629, and had been commander of the forces of the United Colonies of New England against the Narragansett Indians in 1645. In 1650 he was chosen one of the Assistants in Massachusetts. It is not known why he removed to Maryland, but the commission is another proof of the Proprietary's desire at this time to cultivate the favor of the Puritan party. Gibbons came to St. Mary's County, and at his death there, in the latter part of the year 1655 or the early part of 1656, he left a widow, who assigned to Baltimore a windmill belonging to her husband, in satisfaction for a debt of £100 sterling.

The second Councilor,[2] commissioned on August 1, 1651, was Job Chandler, a kinsman of Stone and a brother of Richard Chandler, a London merchant. The appointment seems not to have been made because of Baltimore's knowledge of the appointee, but because of recommendations made by Stone and Richard Chandler. In addition to being made Councilor, Chandler was also given the position of receiver general.

The Assembly summoned for January 10, 1650/1, was

---
[1] 3 Md. Arch., Coun., 261; Bozman, II, 411. The Lord Baltimore's Case, in 1653, appeals to him as a witness for the Proprietary, and states that he was then in England.
[2] 3 Md. Arch., Coun., 263, 299. On Feb. 11, 1653/4, he took the oath of Councilor before Hatton. This was done, probably, because he had not previously taken oath to the Proprietary.

postponed until March 11, when the two houses assembled. Unfortunately the proceedings are lost. Only three acts were passed:[1] one revising the Secretary's and Clerk's fees, which fees Hatton again complained that he had great difficulty in recovering; another providing for a new table of fees for the Surveyor General,[2] and the third arranging for the raising of the levies for the current year in a similar way to that taken in the previous year.[3]

IV. THE PROPRIETOR'S INSTRUCTIONS OF 1651.

Bozman thinks that the Puritans refused or neglected to send any delegates to the Assembly,[4] and that this is probably the cause of the small amount of legislation at the session. Lloyd, the commander of the county, who should have been the returning officer, was doubtless asked so to act, and in reply sent a letter which greatly offended Baltimore,[5] as he showed in the long letter which he wrote Stone on August 26, 1651. Lloyd had written as spokesman "from some lately seated at Anne Arundel," and, as far as we can determine, refused to return burgesses, on the ground of "some reports in those parts of a dissolution or resignation" of Baltimore's patent, "which might perhaps make them doubtful what to do, till they had more certain intelligence" from England. Baltimore had induced their friends in England and particularly Mr. Harrison, their late pastor,[6] who had returned from America, to write to Maryland that the rumors were false, and he hoped that the Providence settlers would give "better satisfaction of their intention and integrity" toward him, "not only by conforming themselves with the rest of the inhabitants to the general government of that Province under which they did voluntarily put themselves, but also by concurring in all reasonable

---

[1] 1 Md. Arch., Ass., 311. See Kilty, 84.
[2] 1 Md. Arch., Ass., 312.
[3] Charles County is to have one or two representatives, 1 Md. Arch., Ass., 313.
[4] Bozman, II, 413.
[5] 1 Md. Arch., Ass., 327.
[6] Bozman, II, 416.

things with us for the public peace and happiness of that Province, as well as for the firm establishment and preservation" of the Proprietary's rights. Their own burgesses had consented to the laws of 1650, which were fundamental for the Province. "Government divided in itself must needs bring confusion," and if the Puritans will not yield to admonition, Baltimore must use his "authority, with the assistance of well affected persons, to compel such factious and turbulent spirits to a better compliance with the lawful government." Furthermore, if the English inhabitants of any part of Maryland refuse to send burgesses to any future Assembly, the other members are directed to proceed with the business of the session in spite of the refusal, and to fine those "refusers or neglecters according to their demerits." If they persist in their refusal or neglect after the Governor admonish them, they shall be declared enemies and rebels.

The reports that Baltimore's charter was shortly to be taken away by the Commonwealth, or that Davenant had been appointed Governor of Maryland by the King, may have reached Virginia and have been the cause of Sir William Berkeley's venturing to authorize Edmund Scarborough of Accomac to seat Palmer's Island in the mouth of the Susquehanna and to trade with the Indians in and through Maryland.[1] Baltimore could not understand "so strange an usurpation" of his rights, and directed Stone to seize Scarborough's men, boats, and goods if he endeavored to exercise the powers of the grant, and to proceed against him according to the laws.

A number of other matters were discussed by Baltimore in this letter.[2] Owing to the loss of records in Ingle's rebellion, he heard that there was no enrollment of divers patents of land, and to prevent the lawsuits which might follow in case the patents themselves should be lost, he ordered Stone to issue a proclamation requiring all persons

---
[1] 1 Md. Arch., Ass., 328; Bozman, II, 417; Davis, 106.
[2] Bozman, II, 418; 1 Md. Arch., Ass., 329.

to present their patents to the Surveyor General, who must make a list of them. No such proclamation remains on the record, and it is doubtful if the Proprietary's laudable directions were carried out, owing to the troubled times which followed.

Baltimore's wise policy is seen clearly in his direction[1] that a tract of eight or ten thousand acres, called " Chaptico, in the head of Wicomico River," be created into a manor by the name of Calverton for the benefit of Indian tribes, namely, the " Mattapanians, the Wicomicons, the Patuxents, the Lamasconsons, the Kighahnixons, and the Chopticons," who have expressed a desire to " put themselves under our protection and to have a grant from us " of that land. It is less than twenty years from the settlement of the Province when we find these aborigines suing for protection and land from the Proprietary, who had denied from the first their right to sell land without his warrant. Probably these tribes had been harassed by the Susquehannocks and wished the aid of the English. The tribes had formerly dwelt in the vicinity of St. Mary's, and had been " not only always well affected unto " the English settlers, but also " willing to submit themselves " to Baltimore's government. Their settlement on this manor " may be a means not only to bring them to civility but also to Christianity and may, consequently, be as well an addition of comfort and strength to the English inhabitants, as a safety and protection to those Indians." Robert Clarke, the Surveyor General, was appointed steward of the manor, to hold the manor courts and grant as copyholds to the Indians for one, two, or three lives any part of the manor save one thousand acres of demesne lands reserved for the Proprietary. No copyhold estate could exceed fifty acres, save those granted to the Werowance or chief of each of the six tribes, who might have two hundred acres. The rent was at the rate of one shilling sterling per fifty acres, and the steward might also fix services to be rendered by the copyholders. It was a

---

[1] Bozman, II, 420; 1 Md. Arch., Ass., 330.

The Proprietor's Instructions of 1651. 51

curious attempt to introduce feudalism among the redmen, and although it failed the plan shows Baltimore's kind purpose.

In the last Conditions of Plantation of July 2, 1649, one hundred acres were allowed for each person transported to Maryland, but it was feared that it would be "prejudicial to the general good of that colony" to continue so "great allowance of land"[1] because "the people will be too remote from one another and the whole Province perhaps, in a short time, be taken up by a few people, leaving little or no conveniency for others to come and add strength and comfort." Looking back on these times, the danger of occupying all the land does not seem to have been imminent, yet it led Baltimore to cut the grant down to fifty acres for each person transported after June 20, 1652. It has not been noted by historians that the Conditions of Plantation were among the causes of the lack of villages in early Maryland history, but the extensive grants a man could obtain undoubtedly tempted him to live separately upon them rather than close to his fellows.[2]

The Proprietary was anxious "for the better publication and remembrance of the bounds between Virginia and Maryland and prevention of controversies" about them.[3] He also wished to take no risks about losing territory. Therefore, he required Stone to encourage some English at once to take up land near to the bounds, according to the maps, now lost, which he had sent over about two years since. Two tracts of land are specified, that "which is commonly called the Eastern Shore," and that which lies between the Potomac and the Piscataway Rivers, in which last tract are included Giles Brent's residence called Peace and the country

---

[1] 1 Md. Arch., Ass., 331; Bozman, II, 423.
[2] Bozman thinks that the use of the word "other" instead of "Irish" widens the class of those who might receive grants. In other respects, the Conditions of Plantation of 1649 and the altered oath of fealty are confirmed.
[3] 1 Md. Arch., Ass., 332; Bozman, II, 423. Bozman is quite in the dark here. The records of Stafford County, Virginia, to which President Lyon G. Tyler of William and Mary College called my attention, afford the clue.

of the Doags. In these two tracts an adventurer may still receive one hundred acres for each person transported. This shows that Baltimore thought that Acquia Creek was the true course of the Potomac. A glance at the map shows how different would have been Maryland's boundaries had this contention been successful.

Mitchell was removed from his Councilorship for sedition, adultery, and atheism. To prevent such scandal for the future,[1] the Proprietary directed Stone that, if he found any Councilor, commander of a county, or justice of the peace guilty of like crimes, or twice guilty of "being a usual drunkard, swearer, or curser," the Governor must suspend him from office, appoint another in his stead, and send the proofs of the ill conduct to the Proprietary, who may decide to discharge or restore the person suspended.

Councilors must be diligent in attendance on the Governor at General Assemblies and Provincial Courts, or be fined and have notice of their neglect sent to the Proprietor, that the latter may "put others in their room, who will give better attendance on the public affairs."[2]

The ill affected persons who continued to publish false reports concerning Baltimore and his affairs caused him alarm, lest they should disquiet the minds of the people and infuse jealousies and doubts in the officers.[3] Consequently, he urges upon Stone the use of his best endeavors to suppress such rumors, to find out the authors, and to cause them to be punished. Further, he recommends the General Assembly to pass a law like the English one, "for the punishment of all such as shall publish false news, to the disturbance of the minds of the people." It is interesting to notice that Baltimore has entirely relinquished to the Assembly the right of the initiative in lawmaking. Rumors of

---

[1] 1 Md. Arch., Ass., 333; Bozman, II, 427.
[2] Bozman, II, 428; 1 Md. Arch., Ass., 334.
[3] 1 Md. Arch., Ass., 335; Bozman, II, 428. Bozman says that the common law gave the right to punish spreaders of false news to the King as part of the jura regalia, but that Baltimore did not suppose that the statutes which confirmed the common law rule extended to Maryland.

gross falsity, alas, continued to be spread through the Province long after Cecilius's death. This long letter, or declaration, was ordered by Baltimore to be read before the General Assembly, as had been done in the case of his letter of August, 1650, and to be published in the usual places of publishing the Proprietary's "ordinances and edicts."

V. THE COMMISSIONERS OF PARLIAMENT OF 1651.

The English Parliament, on October 3, 1650, passed an ordinance forbidding all trade or intercourse with Virginia and the West Indies for their "divers acts of Rebellion," and providing "that the Council of State shall have power to send ships to any of the plantations aforesaid, and to grant commissions to such persons as they shall think fit, to enforce all such to obedience, as stand in opposition to the Parliament, and to grant pardons, and settle governors in the said islands, plantations and places, to preserve them in peace, until the Parliament take further order."[1] No steps were taken under this power for a year after it was given, until on September 26, 1651, Captain Robert Dennis, Mr. Richard Bennett, Mr. Thomas Stagg, and Captain William Claiborne were appointed Commissioners "for the reducing of Virginia and the inhabitants thereof to their due obedience to the Commonwealth of England."[2] Although Maryland was not included in the colonies named in the ordinance of 1650, yet the Council of State seems not to have questioned that power had been given them to "enforce" Maryland "to obedience," if such enforcement were necessary. In the year between the passage of the ordinance and the instructions to the Commissioners all men

---

[1] Bozman, II, 413.
[2] 3 Md. Arch., Coun., 265; Virginia Magazine of History and Biography, XVII, 282. On Bennett see Virginia Magazine of History and Biography, III, 53, and New England Historical and Genealogical Register, January, 1894. He was born about 1622 and died about 1674. Claiborne is discussed by J. E. Cooke in Magazine of American History, X, 83; see also Virginia Magazine of History and Biography, I, 313, and Neill, Terra Mariae, 93.

in Great Britain had been occupied with the Scotch war, until Cromwell's "crowning mercy," the Battle of Worcester, fought on September 3, had overthrown definitely the royal party and firmly established the Commonwealth. The next step was to cut off the trade of the colonies with the Dutch, which was attempted by the passage, on October 9, 1651, of the first of those statutes which we call the Navigation Acts. More important was it to reduce to obedience to the Commonwealth such colonies as the Old Dominion, which still held fast to the monarchical cause.[1]

Baltimore's defender tells us that in the draft of the instructions to Dennis and the others[2] "Maryland was, at first, inserted to be reduced as well as Virginia." Baltimore, however, was able to satisfy the committee, by the testimony of "all the merchants that traded" to Maryland, that this Province "was not in opposition to the Parliament," that Stone "was generally known to have been always zealously affected to the Parliament, and that divers of the Parliament's friends were, by the Lord Baltimore's especial directions, received into Maryland and well treated there, when they were fain to leave Virginia for their good affections to the Parliament." As a result, in the presence of many of the merchants and Dennis and Stagg of the Commissioners,[3] Maryland was stricken from the instructions and ships were permitted to trade there, while none were allowed to go to Virginia. In the body of the instructions, however, was this ambiguous direction, that "upon your arrival at Virginia, you . . . shall use your best endeavors to reduce all the plantations within the Bay of Chesapeake to their due obedience to the Parliament." While Maryland had ceased to be a part of Virginia since the granting of the charter in 1632, from a geographical point of view its plantations were clearly "within the Bay of Chesapeake,"[4] and from

---
[1] Langford, A Just and Cleere Refutation; Bozman, II, 429.
[2] The Lord Baltimore's Case.
[3] See The Lord Baltamore's printed Case Uncased and Answered, 18, for another text of instructions.
[4] The Lord Baltimore's Case artfully says, "Some part of Maryland, where Baltimore's chief colony is settled being within that Bay."

that fact came dire consequences. After referring to the ordinance of 1650, the instructions state that a fleet is now ready, under Dennis's command, to accomplish the purposes of that ordinance, and they direct the Commissioners, who are appointed for "the management of that service, to repair on board the Ship John, or the Guiney Frigate," and sail for Virginia. To reduce the plantations there two or more of the Commissioners must act together, and Captain Dennis must be one of the majority, if he be present. In his absence Captain Edmund Curtis of the *Guiney Frigate* is empowered to take charge of the fleet and to serve as Commissioner. The Commissioners might pardon the inhabitants who should submit, and must "use all acts of hostility that lies in your power" if they refuse to yield. After the settlers yield, the Commissioners shall administer an oath to them, "to be true and faithful to the Commonwealth of England as it is now established," and then shall supervise the election of burgesses for an Assembly by those who have taken the oath. They "shall cause all writs, warrants, and other process whatsoever to be issued forth . . . in the name of the keepers of the Liberty of England by authority of Parliament."[1]

The three Commissioners from England[2]—Dennis, Stagg, and Curtis—sailed from England shortly after receiving their commission, with a small fleet of ships belonging to the

---
[1] Bozman, II, 465; see 301, 636, for earlier ordinance of Parliament of Jan. 23, 1646/7, concerning the several plantations of Virginia, Bermudas, Barbadoes, and other places of America which have been beneficial to England, so that goods are permitted to be exported thither for three years without tax (save to Newfoundland), and persons transported thence from England must be registered in a book at the custom house by the person transporting them. No children, apprentices, or servants may be taken without the consent of their parents or masters, of which the Governor of each plantation must return a certificate within a year. No plantation may allow its goods to be exported to any foreign ports except in English bottoms, on penalty of loss of the benefit of the ordinance and payment of custom as merchants do to French, Spanish, and other foreign ports.

[2] Bozman, II, 435; Langford, A Just and Cleere Refutation; The Lord Baltimore's Case. Hammond, in Leah and Rachel, says, "Not religion nor punctilios, but that sweet, that rich, that large country they aimed at."

English merchants trading to Virginia, "who had engaged to assist with their ships in the reducement" of that Province. On the ships were embarked a regiment of seven hundred men and about one hundred and fifty prisoners taken at the battle of Worcester, and transported so as to be sold into service in Virginia. The fleet sailed by way of the West Indies, and at Barbadoes they aided Sir George Ayscue to reduce that island. Thence the expedition sailed to Virginia, but on the way Captain Dennis and Captain Stagg were cast away in the ship *John,* "the admiral of the fleet," and with them the original commission was lost. Captain Curtis, in the *Guiney Frigate,* arrived safely in Virginia with a copy of the instructions, and calling upon the two American Commissioners, Bennett and Claiborne, to assist him, proceeded to reduce Virginia about the end of February. Sir William Berkeley yielded on March 12, 1651/2, and it is said that Captain Stone "did actually assist" the Commissioners in their efforts at Jamestown.[1] Stone's temporizing policy failed, however, to avert a visit from the Commissioners to his Province. From "aboard the *Guiney Frigate* in Maryland" they wrote this report to England,[2] on March 24, 1651/2: "We are now come to Maryland which, being a plantation within the Bay of Chesapeake, we apprehended it our duty to see the Laws of the Commonwealth of England to be put in execution here, by tendering the Engagement and requiring them to give out Process in the name of the Keepers of the Liberty of England by authority of Parliament and not in the name of the Lord Proprietor, as they have been wont to act and now do. We should warily decline anything that may prejudice the Lord Baltimore in his just rights."

After the three "Commissioners of the Council of State for the Commonwealth of England" came to St. Mary's, on March 29, 1652, they removed Governor, Secretary, and

---
[1] The Lord Baltimore's Case says that Stone furnished assistance and supply of victuals, but Virginia and Maryland denies this.
[2] Virginia Magazine of History and Biography, XI, 34.

Council from[1] office and appointed a new Council of which Robert Brooke was to be the chief, and in which Job Chandler, alone of the Proprietary Councilors, was retained. The new members were Colonel Francis Yardley, Captain Edward Windham, Mr. Richard Preston, and Lieutenant Richard Banks. The Proprietary Councilors had refused to make writs run in the name of the Keepers of the Liberties of England as "inconsistent with the patent of the Lord Proprietor's and their oaths made to him." The Commissioners thereupon decided that obedience to their commissions and the preservation of the honor of the Commonwealth, for settling Maryland in due obedience and peace, demanded a change of administration, "until the Council of State's further pleasure be known." They also demanded that the Governor's commission be given them, and that all the records be delivered into the hands of the new Council. It was ordained that at least two of the new Councilors, of whom Brooke should be one,[2] should hold Provincial Courts, and an Assembly was summoned to meet on June 24. For the election of burgesses to this Assembly only such freemen should vote as had taken an engagement to the Commonwealth.

According to Langford, Stone and the rest of the Proprietary's Council "declared that they did in all humility submit themselves to the government of the Commonwealth of England," but desired to be excused from making writs run in the name of the Keepers of the Liberties of England instead of the Proprietary, as they conceived "the parliament intended not to divest the Lord Baltimore of his right in his province and that they understood out of England that the council of State intended not that the alteration should be made in Maryland." "The king's name hath never been used heretofore," they continued, "in the said writs, but they have always been in the name of the Lord Proprietary, according to the privileges of his Patent ever since the

---

[1] 3 Md. Arch., Coun., 271; Bozman, II, 439; Strong, Babylon's Fall.
[2] Balch, Brooke Family of Whitchurch, Hampshire, England, 16.

beginning of this plantation. The act in England for changing of the forms of writs, declared only that in such writs and processes, wherein the King's name was formerly used, the Keepers of the Liberties of England should for the future be put instead thereof. The continuing of the writs in the Proprietary's name is essential to his interest in the Province and therefore we cannot, without breach of trust, concur to any such alteration."

Langford wisely comments on this proceeding that "Mr. Bennett and Captain Claiborne took upon them an authority much contrary to the intention of the Council of State and indeed much contrary to common sense and reason."

After the "reducement" of Maryland, both Stone and Hatton became private citizens, but the latter retained enough of favor with the new Council to have them vote, on April 22, that any inhabitant of the Province whom Hatton should select might collect, or levy by execution, the fees due him.[1] By this time the Commissioners had returned to Virginia, where, on April 30, Bennett was elected by the Commissioners and burgesses as Governor of the colony for a year and Claiborne was chosen Secretary. Having firmly fixed themselves in position in Virginia, they returned to Maryland, but apparently without Curtis, who may have gone back to England with their report.

Stone was now willing to yield his claim that writs should run in Baltimore's name for the present and "until the pleasures of the State of England be further known," and a proclamation was issued, signed by Bennett and Claiborne and dated June 28, stating that Stone and Hatton were left out of the Council in March upon "some misapprehension" about issuing the writs, but that now Stone, "at the request of the aforesaid Commissioners and the desire of the inhabitants, is content to reassume his former office of

---

[1] Bozman, II, 444. Bozman says that Hatton and Banks (who signed the order with Brooke) were related to each other. In Virginia Magazine of History and Biography, XV, 428, is printed the record of bequest by Hugh Hayes in Presbury, Cheshire, England, dated Apr. 17, 1637, "to the son of my cousin Wm. Stone in Va., my godson."

The Commissioners of Parliament of 1651. 59

Governor and act according" to the proclamation issued in March. Stone, Hatton, Brooke, and Captain John Price are all reinstated in office. Windham and Banks are left out of the Council, but Yardley and Preston are continued. The way in which the Commissioners set up and knocked down Councilors is most interesting. It was now felt that "the Government is so settled, as is known to be to the good liking of the inhabitants," and "for that and several other reasons" the Commissioners saw no "absolute necessity" for an Assembly at the present time, and so revoked the call.[1]

On the day of the reinstatement Stone held a court, at which all of his six Councilors except Price were present.[2] The chief matter before them was a proposed peace with the Susquehannock Indians, the conclusion of which would "tend very much to the safety and advantage of the inhabitants here, if advisedly affected," and which the Indians were said to have a long time desired and much pressed. Bennett, with at least two of the following men, namely, Lloyd, Captain William Fuller, Thomas Marsh, and Leonard Strong, was appointed to treat with the Indians and endeavor to conclude a league with them. The Commissioners were also directed to examine into the conduct of Captain Vaughan, against whose commandership of Kent Island complaints had been made by the inhabitants. If the examination showed that Vaughan should be removed, the Commissioners were empowered to do so and appoint Mr. Thomas Marsh, or some other fitting person, as commander in his room. We have no record that the Commissioners ever examined into these complaints against Vaughan, which were said to be of long standing, the complainants having several times attended the Provincial Court to make their charges against him. At any rate, on December 18 we find Vaughan still serving as commander of the Isle of Kent.[3]

---

[1] It is probable that writs of election were never issued for this Assembly. 3 Md. Arch., Coun., 275.

[2] 3 Md. Arch., Coun., 276. In H. R. Schoolcraft's History of the Indian Tribes of the United States, VI, 128–146, is found an account of the Susquehannocks or Andastes or Minquas or Conestogas, and of the Nanticokes or Conoys or Tochwoghs.

[3] Bozman, II, 453.

The five Commissioners went north to the Severn River[1] and there met an equal number of Indian chieftains, and made a treaty, which was witnessed by William Lawson and Jafer Peter for the Swedes Governor. This last fact lends color to the story that the Swedes were in alliance with the Susquehannocks. The terms of the peace[2] were that the English title was acknowledged to all land north of the Patuxent River and south of Palmer's Island and the North East River, "except the isle of Kent and Palmer's Island, which belongs to Captain Claiborne." On Palmer's Island, however, either English or Indians may build a house or fort for trade.

It is curious that Claiborne interfered so little in the affairs of Maryland after the Puritan ascendancy was established. Bozman surmises, and lack of evidence renders only a surmise possible, that Claiborne was content with collecting quit rents from the people of Kent and permitted the government of the island to be carried on by the Maryland authorities, and it is certain that the civil authority on the island was subordinate to that of the Province during the whole of the period. Palmer's Island must have been abandoned at the time of the treaty, and probably Berkeley's grant of it had not been availed of. After fixing the boundaries, which left in the Indians' hands the country between the North East and Susquehanna Rivers, the treaty went on to provide for mutual reparation and satisfaction for future injuries done, for mutual return of fugitives, for which return a reasonable payment should be made, and for twenty days' warning before war should be begun. Both Indians and English must carry the tokens now exchanged between the parties whenever they have business with each other. While upon these expeditions the Indians shall come

---

[1] Tradition says that the meeting was held under the poplar tree on the St. John's College grounds, in Annapolis; see J. W. Randall, 19.
[2] 3 Md. Arch., Coun., 277; Bozman, II, 449. Bennett was now Governor of Virginia, but acted with the other Treaty Commissioners, doubtless as one of the Parliamentary Commissioners. South of the Patuxent was not Susquehannock territory. The Indian signers were Sawahegeh, Aurotaurogh, Scarhuhadih, Ruthcuhogah, and Wathetdianeh.

by water and not by land, and not more than eight or ten in number at one time, to avoid danger of trouble.

VI. THE PROPRIETOR'S STRUGGLE IN ENGLAND TO RETAIN HIS PROVINCE.

Among the English State papers we find in the summer of 1652 an anonymous series of reasons why it was well to keep the government of the Province divided from that of Virginia,[1] and a petition was presented by Thomas Harrison in behalf of "some well affected inhabitants of Virginia and Maryland."

In 1653 there was published anonymously "The Lord Baltimore's Case," to which were appended the anonymous reasons above referred to and a copy of the commission from "the late King's eldest son to Mr. William Davenant to dispossess the Lord Baltimore" of Maryland, "because of his adherence to the Commonwealth." After claiming that the charter of Maryland had been granted to prevent the Dutch and Swedes from encroaching on Virginia, and referring to the expenditure of £20,000 by the Proprietary and of as much more by his friends on the Province where two of his brothers have died, the pamphlet gives an account of the action of the Parliamentary Commissioners, Bennett and Claiborne, and then tells us what had happened

---

[1] 3 Md. Arch., Coun., 279, 280. The arguments are: (1) that the Commonwealth may control two colonies easier than one large one; (2) that in case of a defection of either colony the well affected may flee into the other; (3) that there will be a rivalry between the colonies to satisfy better the Commonwealth and the planters; (4) that Baltimore's estate and residence in England give better assurance of his loyalty than the Commonwealth could have from those whose interests were wholly in America; (5) that Baltimore pays the Deputy Governor's salary and thus saves the colonists from that expense; (6) that if Baltimore should be prejudiced in his right, it would be a great discouragement to others in foreign plantations to adhere to the Commonwealth, since he ordered his officers to adhere to it, when all the other plantations except New England declared against the Parliament, for which conduct and for receiving the Puritans he was like to be deprived of his interests by the colony of Virginia and the royalist party. This is printed in The Lord Baltimore's Case. The petition is found in Virginia Magazine of History and Biography, XVII, 286.

in England thereafter.[1] Samuel Matthews of Virginia had come to England in behalf of that colony, and Baltimore, with twenty "considerable Protestant adventurers and planters to and in Maryland, who were always well affected," signed a petition on August 31, 1652, against the reincorporation of Maryland into Virginia, from which province Maryland had been separate for over twenty years, and for the reinstatement of the Proprietary officials. A member of the House of Commons produced some papers sent by the Puritan party in Maryland, in the hope that they would show that Baltimore had forfeited his patent, or at least that his authority was not "fit to be allowed" by Parliament. The House then referred the matter to the Committee on the Navy, before which Baltimore appeared, showing his patent and claiming that the present inhabitants of Virginia never had any right to the territory of Maryland.[2] One of the committee submitted exceptions against the patent and Baltimore's proceedings under it, to which he replied. After some debate, the committee decided to deliver no opinion in the matter, but to refer it to a subcommittee, from which it should be reported to the grand committee and by them to the House.[3]

Before this report was made, in all probability the pamphlet was issued, in the hope of influencing public opinion. In addition to "the pretended injury done the Virginians" by the Maryland charter and that done Claiborne by dispossessing him of Kent, it was alleged that the patent constituted an hereditary monarchy in Maryland inconsistent with the Commonwealth, and that Baltimore

---

[1] See also Langford, A Just and Cleere Refutation. Strong, in Babylon's Fall, admits that the Puritans had appealed to England about the oath, and that their appeal had "depended four years without hearing."

[2] See Virginia and Maryland. "[Lord Baltimore's] Reason of State concerning Maryland," Virginia Magazine of History and Biography, XVII, 288.

[3] In Virginia and Maryland it is stated that Claiborne's Kent settlement overruled the hactenus inculta clause, and that the Virginia patent was not vacated on the record of the Rolls Office, and therefore, when it was taken out again by Baltimore's enemies in 1640 under the broad seal, it overthrew his charter.

The Proprietor's Struggle in England. 63

had shown disloyalty to the Commonwealth by consenting in 1650 to the laws passed in 1649, in one of which the late King is styled the "high and mighty Prince, Charles the first of that name, King of England,"[1] and in another of which Baltimore is given customs duty on tobacco shipped from Maryland for any other port "than His Majesty's," by which he acknowledged Charles II as King. Baltimore's advocate answers these new charges, stating that a monarchical government, subordinate to a commonwealth, is consistent with it, as is seen by the kings tributary to Rome and by the lords of manors in England, whose writs yet run in their own names and to whom their tenants take oaths of fealty. Baltimore's powers, greater than those of the English lords of manor, would not be convenient in England, but are necessary for the undertakers of plantations in so remote and wild a place as Maryland, and his laws there must be consonant to reason, not repugnant to those of England, and made with the consent of a majority of the freemen. No one would be so indiscreet as to undertake a plantation if, after all his charge and hazard, "such necessitous, factious people, as usually new plantations consist of for the most part," men sent thither by him and often at his charge, should have power to dispose of all his estate there without his consent, for he might thus be ruined before the English authority on an appeal might be at leisure to relieve him. It is true that Baltimore is a Roman Catholic, but the laws against recusants do not reach into America, and it is far better that he possess the country than Indian kings or foreigners, such as the Dutch and Swedes. None are compelled to go to Maryland or stay there, but all know beforehand the terms of settlement, and the people of the Province in general, both Protestants and Roman Catholics, are pleased with their government.[2] To the complaint that his laws recognized Charles II by referring to Charles I, the reply was made that in so speaking, as of first-born sons,

---
[1] I can find no such phrase in the Acts of 1649.
[2] A petition with ten signatures against Baltimore in the name of the inhabitants of Maryland is said to be either fictitious or "signed by some few obscure factious fellows."

James I, or the first year of a reign, no second is implied, but the "word first hath relation to time past," and that, when the laws were passed in April, 1649, the people in Maryland did not know of the King's death, but referred to Charles I by the term "His Majesty." Ships return to England from Maryland in February, March, and April, and go thither in September, October, and November, so no news had come into the Province of the King's death.[1]

In the pamphlet which the Puritan party issued two years later in reply to "The Lord Baltimore's Case," and which they entitled "Virginia and Maryland," answers are given to Baltimore's advocate and many more charges are made. As Claiborne had settled the country, it was not uncultivated when the Maryland charter was issued. The Virginia charter has been revived, therefore the Maryland one is dead. Baltimore has prevented the Virginians from enjoying the fur trade and thrown it into the hands of Dutch and Swedes. He enforced illegal oaths to maintain himself as Proprietary and to protect the Roman Catholics in the free exercise of their religion, sending out instructions therefor, as if he were king. He carried on the government, not naming the sovereign authority of England. He took away most of the Virginia territory by his charter, yet has but few planters and these mostly employed in tobacco-raising in a small corner of Maryland—men who sell arms to the Indians almost as openly as the Swedes and Dutch.

The Province is a nursery for Jesuits, and admits Papists and Irishmen.[2] His first Governors were Romanists.

---

[1] The Lord Baltimore's Case, concerning the Province of Maryland adjoining to Virginia in America, with full and clear answers to all material objections touching his rights, jurisdictions and proceedings there, and certain reasons of State why Parliament should not impeach the same, unto which is also annexed a true copy of a commission from the late King's eldest son to Mr. William Davenant to dispossess the Lord Baltimore of the said Province because of his adherence to the Commonwealth. 1653. This pamphlet is reprinted in Maryland Historical Magazine, IV, 171.

[2] Of the Irish two thousand came, and it had been said of them, "Those Irish would not leave a Bible in Maryland." The Puritans point to the troubles with Claiborne, to Leonard Calvert's commission from the King, to Greene's proclamation of Charles II.

There is a chapel to St. Ignatius and his feast-day is kept as a holiday, while the Protestants are miserably disturbed, or enforced by subtile practices to turn Papists. He has made laws not agreeable to those of England, divided the legislature into two houses, and established a Privy Council of State (to which he calls whom he will) not mentioned in his charter. He permits Dutch, French, or Italians to plant and enjoy equal privileges with the British and Irish. There are no appeals from his courts and the judges often decide their own cases. Baltimore has made no great adventures on the Province. The assistance of Virginia, whence Maryland was chiefly planted, was essential to its subsistence, yet Virginia has found the northern Province continually inviting and entertaining runaway slaves and debtors. When one reads this long list of complaints, the conclusion seems to be that the writer wished Virginia and Maryland to be united into one Puritan-ruled Province and took any arguments which he thought would advance that purpose.

VII. GOVERNOR STONE, 1652–3.

Though the difficulties with the Susquehannocks were settled, other Indians gave much trouble. Against the Yoacomico and Matchoatick tribes who dwelt on the south side of the Potomac, Governor Stone issued a proclamation on August 9, 1652.[1] They hunt in St. Mary's and Charles Counties, and destroy game, hogs, and cattle. Also, their insolencies are not to be endured. Therefore the inhabitants are forbidden to entertain or trade with these Indians, "excepting any Indian cowkeeping youth," and the Indians are given fair warning to be gone. If they do not heed this warning, Captain John Price shall levy soldiers and drive them from the Province.

A more serious difficulty occurred in November[2] when

---
[1] 3 Md. Arch., Coun., 281.
[2] 3 Md. Arch., Coun., 279. Henry Morgan, John Phillips, Philip Conner, Thos. Ringgold. Bozman, II, 419, 455. In 1648 a writer reported but twenty men on the island and the fort pulled down. If this were so, the settlers were clearly too weak to resist an Indian attack. Bozman conjectures that the Susquehanna treaty ceding the Eastern Shore may have aroused the Nanticokes.

four of the Commissioners of Kent petitioned Stone and the Council to consider their "deplorable condition and take some speedy course for the suppressing of these heathens." The Eastern Shore Indians had killed three Englishmen on the island, burned a dwelling-house, continually killed hogs, and daily came about the houses with guns. They are said to have much ammunition which they have bought, taken from "Capt. Guignis his Rack" and from a Dutch sloop which they have lately seized, with forty-nine guns besides very much powder and shot, "so that they are very strong, bold, and insolent." For fear of them many Englishmen have already left their plantations and others plan to desert the island. On November 25 the Council received this petition.[1] Stone, Yardley, Price, Hatton, and Chandler were present, and called upon the advice and assistance of several others, among whom was Captain Thomas Cornwallis, who had not recently been prominent in the Province. After consideration, it was ordered that every seventh man in the Province be pressed to raise a force for a march against these Eastern Shore Indians. The sheriffs of the various counties are to manage the levy, from which Councilors, Commissioners, and other officers are exempt, and to procure boats for transportation of the expedition.[2] The six men not pressed must victual the seventh for an expedition of twenty days from the time of meeting at the rendezvous on Kent Island, and must provide him with a gun and ammunition. On December 20 the levies from St. Mary's and the Patuxent must meet at Mattapany upon the latter river. Then the Governor shall appoint them a commander who must lead the expedition across to the rendezvous on Kent Island on December 30. There Captain William Fuller shall take command of the whole force.[3] The Indian

---

[1] 3 Md. Arch., Coun., 282. We have no other account of the capture of the Dutch sloop.
[2] No exceptions of persons allowed here.
[3] Wm. Thompson, servant to John Jarboe, must be pressed, and the necessary tools for his fixing of guns must be procured from John Dandy.

prisoners who may be taken are to be divided among the six men who equip the expedition,[1] while "all other purchase or plunder, whether of corn or otherwise," shall be divided amongst the commander and soldiers. Four days later Stone issued a commission to Fuller as commander in chief, and directed him to have forces levied in Anne Arundel County. After leaving the Kent Island rendezvous, Fuller, with his troops, is directed to march against any Indians on the Eastern Shore within the limits of Maryland, to make war upon them, and kill or take them prisoners in his discretion.[2] He might put his prisoners " to death by the law of war, or save them" at his pleasure, and when we find such laws of war upheld by Europeans, we can hardly condemn the cruelty of their Indian foes. Fuller might pursue his adversaries, if occasion arise in the war, " beyond the bounds" of Maryland, as was done by Jackson in his pursuit of the Seminoles into Florida in 1818.[3] On the same day on which Fuller's commission was issued Stone signed orders to the sheriffs to muster the men.[4] Kent should provide one sloop, Anne Arundel as many sloops as necessary, and St. Mary's, Charles, and the north side of the Patuxent two more. On the next day he issued orders to the constables in the three last named divisions of the Province to aid the sheriffs, and on December 2 he ordered[5] Preston, who is spoken of as " Commander on the North side of Patuxent River," "to appoint officers to raise men on either side" of that river. In spite of these elaborate preparations, the expedition never set forth. Stone's letter reached Fuller on December 6, and when Fuller went among the Puritans, he found them "wholly disaffected, not to the

---

[1] Bozman (II, 458) points out that at that time it was held that the victor, having the right to put a captured enemy to death, must have a right to enslave him as a humane commutation, and that Grotius held this view.
[2] 3 Md. Arch., Coun., 285. Bozman (II, 459) has an interesting note concerning Wicocomoco Point, mentioned in the commission to Fuller as the southernmost point of the Province.
[3] Bozman, II, 459.
[4] 3 Md. Arch., Coun., 286.
[5] 3 Md. Arch., Coun., 288.

thing," which would "be of good use, if wisely managed," but to "the time of the year." They said that it would probably "be dangerous for their health, first, in regard [to] the want of necessaries, as also want of vessels fit to transport them and, next, that it is possible they may be frozen into the rivers and so expose themselves to more dangers through cold and want of necessary provisions than by the enemies." Furthermore, Fuller found that the Western Shore Indians knew of the proposed expedition before he received his commission, and it were well to put off the march for this reason and to make an order against revealing the Council's designs to any Indians. Therefore Fuller wrote Stone, on the thirteenth of December, advising that a delay be made until the "extremity of the winter be past." Fuller does not wish to seem "to slight the power God hath placed over me, but am ready to submit to it and that, really, as for myself, I am ready, both now and at any other time, to do yourself and the country all possible service." As a proof of this readiness, he plans, "if weakness of body prevent not," to give the Islanders "a visit and advise with them," and will "readily assist them, if occasion be offered, with men or otherwise."[1]

When Fuller's letter reached Stone, he issued a proclamation, dated December 18, giving up the expedition for the present, on the grounds of the reasons which Fuller named and because the soldiers had great want of apparel and other necessaries.[2]

On the day on which the last named proclamation was issued Stone issued a second one,[3] revoking the permission to Lloyd and Vaughan, which had been given on July 29, 1650, to grant warrants for land. The transmission of the warrants and of the certificates of survey had been neglected, to the prejudice of the Proprietary's rents and to the

---

[1] 3 Md. Arch., Coun., 289.
[2] 3 Md. Arch., Coun., 290.
[3] 3 Md. Arch., Coun., 290. The publication of Land Notes 1634–1655, being abstracts of the entries in the Land Office Records, was begun in Maryland Historical Magazine, V, 166, and continued on pages 261 and 365.

wrong of the Secretary's office. To prevent this, the power is revoked, and Vaughan and Lloyd must send transcripts of all the land records of their counties to the Secretary at once. Clarke, the Surveyor General, is also ordered to send speedily to the Secretary all certificates of survey not yet returned, and to survey no land in future for any one without a special warrant from the Governor or the Proprietary.[1] The lack of return from these officers was a cause of trouble in the Province for a century afterwards by making titles uncertain.

In the autumn of 1652[2] the first settlement was made within the present limits of Baltimore County. The Surveyor General landed from his shallop on the shores of the Patapsco River, and laid out on November 19 five tracts of land on the south bank. Crossing over to the north bank, he laid out there on November 20 six hundred acres for Thomas Sparrow, under the name of Northconton, and one thousand one hundred and fifty acres for Thomas Thomas and William Batten jointly, under the name of Old Road. Two days later two more tracts were laid out by the Surveyor General before he left the river: one of four hundred and twenty-five acres for Richard Owens and one of three hundred acres for Augustin Gillett. Of the grantees who pushed thus far into the wilderness, Thomas Sparrow is still remembered in the name of the "busy industrial town" of Sparrow's Point.

The troubles with the internal government and with the Indians had probably been partly the cause of a scarcity of corn, which led Stone to issue a proclamation, on January

---

[1] His previous irregular and unwarrantable proceedings had occasioned much trouble and inconvenience. Bozman (II, 461) thinks that the failure to transmit these warrants was due to disloyalty to the Proprietary, but the circumstances are scarcely clear enough to prove his point. He thinks Lord Propy. v. Jennings, 1 H. & McH. 92, was the result of Lloyd's and Clarke's carelessness. Kilty, 76, April 5, 1653. Stone authorized Hatton to grant land warrants on the Patuxent at a convenient distance from any Indian town, in spite of former directions to the contrary.

[2] C. W. Bump, "The First Grants on the Patapsco," Maryland Historical Magazine, III, 53. The early death in April, 1908, of this faithful scholar is much to be regretted.

24, 1652/3, that no one should transport from the Province, until Michaelmas next, without a special license from Stone, any corn which he might buy from Indians inhabiting within the Province.[1] This proclamation shows clearly that the yield of the planters' corn-fields was not as yet sufficient for their use and that they were still largely dependent upon the Indians' crops, though nearly twenty years had passed since the first settlement. The free trade with the Dutch had probably been an incitement to the cultivation of tobacco, and induced the planters to neglect the cultivation of cereals. The Dutch trade was now cut off, however, for Parliament on October 9, 1651, had enacted the earliest of the Navigation Acts, providing "that no merchandise from the plantations" should be imported into England in any but " English-built ships, belonging either to English or English plantation subjects, navigated also by an English commander, and with three fourths of the sailors Englishmen." In 1652 Parliament tried to increase the tobacco monopoly and production in the plantations by passing an act " against planting tobacco in England."

In the spring Indian rumors were heard again, and this time the Indians of the Potomac were the ones feared.[2] Gerard was authorized, on March 24, 1652/3, to use the best means he could to discover their designs, and to go to Port Tobacco, or Chaptico, for that purpose. Cornwallis and Brooke were also consulted. One of Brooke's sons and another man were employed as "intelligencers" among the Indians living upon Patuxent River. If the Mathue Indians should come to trade with the Patuxents, the intelligencers must give notice to Brooke and Preston, who were to apprise Stone so as to arouse the militia under Captain Price to destroy these Indians.

Toward the end of July[3] four Piscataway Indians, two

---

[1] 3 Md. Arch., Coun., 293; Bozman, II, 463.
[2] 3 Md. Arch., Coun., 293; Bozman, II, 467. The Mathue Indians have not been identified.
[3] 10 Md. Arch., Prov. Ct., 293; Davis, 151, 270 (verdict was given on the faith of the jurors).

Governor Stone, 1652–3.

of whom were named Skigh-tam-mongh and Couna-weza, entered Captain Daniel Gookin's house on South River in Anne Arundel County, in which, apparently, were at the time only a negro servant, Jacob Warrow, with his wife, Mary, and their seven-year-old son. The Indians remained in the house for about an hour, and then, as Warrow stooped down, they fell upon him with their tomahawks and killed him. His wife started to flee with the child, but one of the Indians struck her with his tomahawk as she was going out of the door, so that she fell senseless. When she came to herself she saw that her child was killed, but managed to creep into the weeds by the house and watch the Indians pillage the house of guns, powder and shot, wearing apparel and bedclothes, pewter ware and hats. The two Indians named above, one of whom the negress identified as the one who struck her, were found with some of the stolen goods and were delivered to the settlers by "Warcosse, the Emperor." At the trial on September 26, 1653, they admitted that they were present when the man and child were killed, and were tried by a jury of twenty-four of the freemen of St. Mary's County. These brought in a curious verdict that, if the Indians had not consented to the murders, they ought to have withstood their companions or revealed these acts, but "doing neither and receiving stolen goods (as they confess) as hired to conceal it," they were guilty of the murder. The court sentenced them to be hanged, "which execution was performed the same evening accordingly."

On September 26, 1653, Stone adjourned the Provincial Court until December 1; but on November 7 he further postponed it until January 10, as no necessity appeared of holding a court so soon.[1] No English shipping had yet arrived, and, for "divers reasons relating to the public welfare, it were requisite . . . that we received some directions out of England touching the government here, before a General Court." The court was again postponed[2] and met on February 1, 1653–4. The Dutch war raged during this year,

---

[1] 3 Md. Arch., Coun., 294, see 10 Md. Arch., Prov. Ct., 278 and 296.
[2] 10 Md. Arch., Prov. Ct., 309; Bozman, II, 469.

and the overthrow of the Parliamentary government in England by Cromwell, on April 20, 1653, may not have been officially reported owing to the dangers to navigation. Rumors of Cromwell's act had probably come, and may have caused Stone's delay of the meeting of the court until he had definite news as to what the government was in the mother-country.

In July, 1653, Colonel Matthews, the agent for the colony of Virginia, urged the authority of the Commissioners before the Committee of Petitions of Cromwell's first Parliament; but his petition was either dismissed or referred to the Council of State, " as more proper for their consideration."[1]

Before the Provincial Court met, Stone had issued two proclamations.[2] In January he forbade any one to molest Simon Oversey, an Englishman born, and an inhabitant of Maryland and Virginia for several years past, in the following of his lawful occasions of trade, and he refused to intermeddle in the matter of the seizure of a Spanish prize called the *Maid of Gaunt,* taken in the St. George's River[3] by Captain Thomas Webber in the *Mayflower* of London. Stone referred the trial of the business to the London Court of Admiralty, and promised Webber and the merchants on the *Mayflower* that they should not be troubled in their free trade within Maryland in either ship. On June 12 a certificate was given Oversey that Webber had carried out of Maryland in this prize forty-six hogsheads of the former's tobacco, and had refused to submit to a trial of the matter before the Governor and Council.

VIII. STONE'S BREACH WITH THE COMMISSIONERS, 1654.

By February shipping had doubtless come from England, and as a result of the letters and other news received thereby,

---

[1] Langford, A Just and Cleere Refutation; Bozman, II, 470.
[2] 3 Md. Arch., Coun., 298, 306.
[3] The sails of the captured ship were on shore when the ship was seized, and Stone said that he would consider whether they, by statute or justice, were part of the prize and would secure them until he gave a positive answer to the question.

Stone's Breach with the Commissioners. 73

Stone issued a proclamation on February 7,[1] dated, as were all of his, at St. Mary's, "by the special appointment and direction" of the Proprietary. Many have not sued out patents for land, nor taken the oath of fidelity according to the Conditions of Plantation, yet Baltimore will not take advantage of this default, but will allow land claimed under the Conditions of 1649 if the claimants take the oath, sue out the patent, and pay all arrears of rents within three months. If they do not obey this order, they shall be debarred from all rights to the lands so claimed. Four days after this proclamation, Chandler and Clarke took the oath of Councilor to the Lord Proprietary.[2] The latter was now first added to the Council, the former had probably not taken the oath before the Parliamentary Commissioners reduced the government. As the oath contained a clause that the taker would not molest any one, particularly a Roman Catholic, for his religion, the Puritans held that it was in plain words to "countenance and uphold anti-Christ."[3]

Stone took the decisive step of breaking away from the orders of the Parliamentary Commissioners on March 2, 1653/4, when he decreed that writs should "run in the Proprietary's name as heretofore,"[4] inasmuch as this "cannot any ways derogate from our obedience" to the Commonwealth. Stone professed that he was careful not to infringe his engagement to the Commonwealth that he would be true and faithful to the Commonwealth of England as it is now established, without King or House of Lords. He also cautioned the Commissioners of Kent to raise "convenient forces" on the Island to prevent mischief suspected from

---

[1] 3 Md. Arch., Coun., 298; Bozman, II, 473. Bozman remarks that Baltimore's instructions of February 17, 1652/3 (now lost), may have come in this fleet.

[2] 3 Md. Arch., Coun., 299; Bozman, II, 478; 10 Md. Arch., Prov. Ct., 322.

[3] Strong, Babylon's Fall.

[4] 3 Md. Arch., Coun., 300; The Lord Baltamore's printed Case Uncased and Answered, 28, 30, 32; Bozman, II, 478. Browne (Maryland: The History of a Palatinate, 78) holds that Baltimore directed Stone to do this because Cromwell had succeeded to the Protectorate in England. Virginia and Maryland says that it was done by Baltimore's direction.

the Indians. When Stone proclaimed Baltimore, he arranged with two shipmasters whose vessels were in Maryland to fire off pieces of ordnance in celebration of the event.[1]

Colonel Francis Yardley became discontented at this time. He had been placed by Bennett and Claiborne in the Council at the " reducement of the Province." As early as March 4 he was reported to show " contemptuous carriage and demeanor towards the government," and was suspected of intending " to remove his estate out of this Province and to leave his debts and engagements here[2] unsatisfied." To prevent this, a writ was issued by Stone, on March 20, prohibiting Yardley from leaving the Province. It may be, as Bozman points out, that this writ was issued by Stone, in his capacity as Chancellor, to prevent Yardley from removing his property out of the Province.

Just two days before issuing the writ against Yardley, Stone licensed Captain Thomas Adams, mariner,[3] who had lately purchased a plantation in Maryland, to trade for any merchandise not forbidden by the laws with the Swedes " in Delaware Bay, or in any part of this Province, being not enemies to the Commonwealth, as also with any Indians on the Eastern Shore . . . not in open hostility with the inhabitants here." He must take care, however, to keep his vessel well manned and armed, to prevent danger from the Indians. The Statute of 1650 prohibited Indian trade without license, and the Swedish trade must have been considered to be included in the prerogative powers of the Lord Proprietary. New Haveners, Swedes, and Dutchmen were claiming the land on the Delaware and endeavoring to establish colonies there. The history of this contest is a most interesting one, but, though the territory was largely included

---

[1] Hammond, Hammond versus Heamans.
[2] Bozman, II, 478; 3 Md. Arch., Coun., 301. The writ was addressed to Lieutenant Wm. Lewis, George Dolty, or Edmond Lindsay. Deposition that Col. Yardley said that he intended to remove to the southward, and attachment laid on his property in the Province on March 4, 10 Md. Arch., Prov. Ct., 343.
[3] 3 Md. Arch., Coun., 301; Bozman, II, 479.

within Baltimore's patent, the events of the struggle are not properly a part of the history of the Province.[1] In April, Hatton brought in his return of the Dutch customs, which he had received and partly paid to the soldiers,[2] and eighteen receipts were filed from the latter or their assigns. It may be remembered that an act in 1649 provided that all tobacco shipped in Dutch vessels to any other than British ports should pay the Proprietary a duty of ten shillings per hogshead, half of which was to be applied to paying the soldiers who recovered the Province for Baltimore.

Thomas Belcher of Anne Arundel County was licensed to keep an ordinary there, which act showed that Stone resolved to reestablish his authority throughout all the Province.

Cromwell received back the powers of government from the Little or Barebones Parliament on December 12, 1653, and four days later the Council of Officers declared "that the government of the Commonwealth should reside in a single person, that that person should be Oliver Cromwell, Captain General of all the forces in England, Scotland and Ireland, and that his title should be lord protector of the Commonwealth of England, Scotland & Ireland and of the dominions and territories thereunto belonging." In his name should all writs run from that time forth. The news[3] of this event reached Maryland in the spring of 1654 and was hailed with joy by Stone, who saw in it a means to support his conflict with the Commissioners. Therefore, on May 6, he issued a proclamation of the Protectorate, commanding all persons to submit to it. "In commemoration of this solemnity" he made public announcement of the pardon of all crimes except treason, rebellion, or conspiracy against the Lord Proprietary.[4] Persons especially excepted from pardon by Baltimore and those owing forfeitures adjudged to be paid but not yet satisfied were also exempted from the benefits of the proclamation.

---
[1] Bozman, II, 481-492.
[2] 3 Md. Arch., Coun., 302; 10 Md. Arch., Prov. Ct., 345, 372.
[3] Bozman, II, 495.
[4] 3 Md. Arch., Coun., 305; Bozman, II, 498.

76   *Maryland Under the Commonwealth.*

We have not many more glimpses of Stone's governorship. On June 23 we find two depositions on the records concerning the recent execution by the sailors as a witch of one Mary Lee on the voyage of the Ship *Charity* of London, England,[1] and on July 3 Stone, with the advice of his Council, repealed the ordinance of November 21, 1650, which erected Charles County, and erected the territory on both sides of the Patuxent River into Calvert County, of which county Richard Collett was made high sheriff. The reason for this change was that instructions[2] of September 28, 1653, from Baltimore had been received which had "discharged Robert Brooke, Esq. late Commander of Charles County from being of the Council, Conservator, or Justice of the Peace, or Commander of any County." The cause of this displacement we can only surmise, but shall probably state it correctly as the Proprietary's dissatisfaction with Brooke's willingness to act as President of the Council when the reducement of the Province was made by Bennett and Claiborne.

Before issuing his new decree that writs would run in the Proprietary's name, Stone seems to have insisted on the oath of fidelity,[3] and on January 3, 1653/4, Edward Lloyd and seventy-seven householders and freemen from the Severn River, by letter to Bennett and Claiborne, complained of the oath as "not agreeable to the terms on which we came hither, nor to the liberty of our consciences as Christians and free subjects of the Commonwealth of England and, indeed, contrary to the engagement taken thereto." Stone had said that he would seize the lands of all who did not take the oath within three months. The Puritans complained to the Council, but had received an aspersion cast upon them of being factious fellows, instead of an answer which would clear the lawfulness of Baltimore's proceed-

---
[1] 3 Md. Arch., Coun., 306; "Relatio Itineris in Marylandiam," Maryland Historical Society, Fund Publication no. 7, p. 90.
[2] 3 Md. Arch., Coun., 308; Bozman, II, 500. The instructions are lost.
[3] Virginia and Maryland.

Stone's Breach with the Commissioners. 77

ing. They asked for help, believing that the Commonwealth would not expose them to such real bondage as to make them swear absolute subjection to a government where the ministers are bound by oath to countenance and defend the Roman Popish religion and carry on arbitrary power. In answer to this petition Bennett and Claiborne admonished Stone of his error; nevertheless, when the men of Patuxent refused to take the oath, Stone denounced them as seditious and rebellious, and included Bennett and Claiborne under the same charge with other opprobrious terms.

On March 1 Richard Preston and sixty other freemen of Patuxent addressed Bennett and Claiborne, asking protection from the "pride, rage, and insolency of enemies." The writs now run in the Proprietary's name, and an oath is demanded, contrary to the engagement to the Commonwealth and the word of God, for it obliges them to "maintain Popery and a popish Anti-Christian Government, which we dare not do, unless we should be found traitors to our country, fighters against God, and covenant breakers." They wished help, at least until they could appeal to England.

Bennett and Claiborne answered this letter, on March 12, 1653/4, advising and requiring the petitioners to continue in the establishment made by the Parliamentary Commissioners, as no sufficient order from Parliament is known to the contrary, in spite of the pretence of power from Baltimore or his agents. Frequent requests came to Virginia from men of Severn, Patuxent, and Kent for relief, so back into the Province came Bennett and Claiborne.[1] The Parliament from which they derived their authority had expired over a year ago, and no legal authority under which they might act appears, but the fact that writs ran again in the Proprietary's name, that the oath of fidelity to him was demanded from those who took up land in the Province, that the Councilors had to swear not to molest Roman

---
[1] Bozman, II, 501; 3 Md. Arch., Coun., 311; Langford, A Just and Cleere Refutation.

Catholics, that Brooke had been displaced from and Clarke added to the Council, aroused Bennett and Claiborne to action.

About July 10 they "applied themselves"[1] to Stone and his Council, but received what they styled "opprobrious and uncivil language." Stone was also charged by them with mustering his "whole power of men" in arms, intending to surprise the Commissioners by night. Then they went northward across the Patuxent, as they said, "in quiet and peaceable manner, with some of the people of Patuxent and Severn." At Patuxent, on July 15, they issued a proclamation against Stone. Bennett had sent for aid from Virginia, of which colony he was Governor, and Stone was thus between two fires. He, therefore, sent word that the next day he would meet and treat in the woods, to prevent effusion of blood and the ruin of the country, and as a result, on July 20 he "condescended to lay down his power lately assumed from the lord Baltimore and to submit . . . to such government as the commissioners should appoint" under the Protector.[2]

The Commissioners, therefore, on July 22 directed Hatton to deliver the Provincial records to William Durand,[3] the elder of the Puritan settlement, whom they appointed Secretary, and they issued a commission of government which they falsely said was given by them as "Commissioners for his highness, to the reducing and settling the Plantations of Virginia and Maryland" under his obedience. This document refers to the former "reducement," to Stone's return to the use of the oath of fidelity and of the

---

[1] Strong, Babylon's Fall; Bozman, II, 504, 684; 3 Md. Arch., Coun., 311; Virginia and Maryland.
[2] Hammond, Hammond versus Heamans; Virginia and Maryland (Gerard, Hatton, and Scarborough witness his resignation, and Strong calls Scarborough a mischievous instrument of Baltimore).
[3] Davis, 70; Neill, Founders of Maryland, 116. Thomas Marsh was Durand's servant when he came to Maryland. In October, 1651, Durand took up land at the Cliffs for himself, wife, five children, two freemen, and five servants. He had sat under Davenport's preaching in London. A Quaker wrote home in 1658: "Wm. Fuller abides unmoved. I know not but Wm. Durand doth the same" (Neill, Founders of Maryland, 116).

Proprietary's name in writs, and to a lost proclamation, issued by Stone on July 4, charging the Commissioners and those who refused to take the oath of fidelity with drawing away the people and leading them "into sedition, faction, and rebellion against the Lord Baltimore."

Therefore, Stone is deposed, as is his Council, and Captain William Fuller, Richard Preston,[1] William Durand, Edward Lloyd, Captain John Smith, Leonard Strong, John Lawson, John Hatch, Richard Wells, and Richard Ewen are appointed "Commissioners for the well ordering, directing, and governing the affairs of Maryland" under the Protector. Four is to be their quorum, and Fuller, Preston, or Durand must be present at each meeting. They shall issue writs, hold courts, and summon an Assembly to meet on October 20. At the election for this Assembly no one shall vote or be chosen as a member who had "borne arms in war against the Parliament" or who professed the Roman Catholic religion.

The first General Assembly under the Commissioners was held on October 20, 1654, probably at Preston's house near Battletown in Calvert County on the Patuxent River.[2] We have no records of its debates, but possess forty-six brief laws passed at the session. The Assembly seems to have consisted of one house, wherein Fuller had the titular first place and Preston was Speaker. Nine Commissioners and seven other men were present, and three of the latter were afterwards named as Commissioners.[3] Thomas Hatton and

---

[1] See article upon Preston by Samuel Troth in Pennsylvania Magazine of History and Biography, XVI, 207. He probably came to Virginia in 1636, æt. about 22, and to Maryland in 1650, with three sons and two daughters. He was later a Quaker and died in 1666. His son Richard was an Assemblyman from Calvert and Dorchester, and his grandson Samuel removed to Philadelphia.

[2] Glenn, Some Colonial Mansions and Those Who Lived in Them, II, 350. Bozman (II, 507) does not know where Preston lived.

[3] 1 Md. Arch., Ass., 339 ff. All the Commissioners were present but John Lawson. Sampson Waring, James Berry, and Wm. Ewen, who were later Commissioners, were present, as were Thomas Hinson, Joseph Weekes, and Turner and Wade. This is the first Assembly in which members sat for counties.

Job Chandler, who had been chosen burgesses for the county of "St. Mary's and Potomac River," as the Puritans called it, came before the Assembly and refused to sit, because of their oath to Baltimore and for other reasons expressed in a writing, now lost, which they left with Durand, the Secretary. A new writ was issued to the sheriff for a second choice of burgesses, and he shortly returned as unanimously elected Arthur Turner and John Wade, who duly qualified. As Roman Catholics had been disqualified, and as it is probable that some of the Proprietary's adherents did not vote, the unanimity must have been that of a small number of electors. Hatton and Chandler and their constituents were not allowed to go without paying for their loyalty to Baltimore, for the Assembly voted that the charge of the new election should be borne by the County of "Mary's and Potomac," and that, if the fault was in Hatton and Chandler, rather than in the electors, the latter had liberty granted to recover the charge from the former.[1] That means, as Bozman wisely conjectures, that if the two gentlemen, before their election, informed their electors that they could not serve, the expense fell on the county, otherwise it fell on Hatton and Chandler, as caused by their default.

The first law passed[2] was an act of recognition, "in the name of his highness the Lord Protector," acknowledging and freely submitting to the reducing of the Province by Bennett and Claiborne and to the government as it was now settled by commission granted the ten Commissioners. No power from Baltimore or any other should be permitted to alter the government so settled, unless it came from the supreme authority of the Commonwealth, exercised by the Protector. All the inhabitants of the Province were required to declare that they accepted the present government and would be subject thereto. Any one who denied this government, or dared either in words to "traduce, villify or

---

[1] 1 Md. Arch., Ass., 354; Bozman, II, 309.
[2] Bozman, II, 511.

scandalize" it or by action to oppose it, should be accounted an offender against the Protector of the Province. So too any one who published any commission, proclamation, or writ not from the supreme authority above named should be accounted an offender against the public peace.

The Assembly's mind was that any free subject of the Commonwealth[1] should have liberty of petition for redress of grievances and also of propounding things in an orderly manner necessary for the public good. This early suggestion of a popular initiative was doubtless a reminiscence of the early Assemblies, to which all freemen could come.

Next the body turned its attention to religion, and throwing aside Baltimore's enlightened policy of toleration, decreed that none who professed the "Popish religion" could be protected by the laws, but were restrained from the exercise of their faith. Liberty of religion was not to be "extended to popery or prelacy, nor to such as, under the profession of Christ, hold forth and practice licentiousness."[2] Other Christians, though differing in judgment from the Puritans' religion, should be protected in the profession of their faith so long as they "abuse not this liberty to the injury of others." The narrowness of this statute, passed by men who came to Maryland to escape religious persecution, merits all the obloquy which has been cast upon it. Bozman calls our attention to the fact that this act is copied from the instrument of government by which Cromwell had been installed as Protector on December 16, 1653. The gratitude which should have been owed Baltimore was forgotten in religious antipathy. The Assembly also took the pains to repeal the famous act of 1649 concerning religion.[3]

The revolution in the Province is also shown in two other acts,[4] one of which declared null Baltimore's proclamation

---
[1] Why is not the word Province used? 1 Md. Arch., Ass., 340; Bozman, II, 511.
[2] 1 Md. Arch., Ass., 341; Bozman, II, 512.
[3] 1 Md. Arch., Ass., 351.
[4] 1 Md. Arch., Ass., 354; Bozman, II, 515. Claiborne's attainder

commanding that the oath of fidelity be taken to him, while the other ordered that all suits pending in the courts before the "reducement of the Province" should not be affected by that event. This act showed that the Puritans had the honesty not to try to avoid the payment of old debts. The bugbear of the oath of fidelity appears in another law "concerning rights of land." This statute stated that the oath of fealty, required by Baltimore's Conditions of Plantation, is contrary to the laws of England, so that those who have rights to land cannot, without collusion and deceit, apply for patents to the Proprietary's officers.[1] To correct this, "all those, that transport themselves or others into this Province" are decreed to "have a right to land by virtue of their transportation." This right may be entered in the county court, and the owner may also enter a caveat for the particular tract of land which he may take up, which caveat shall take the place of a patent.

Concerning the government of the Province, several statutes were passed. Assemblies[2] should be summoned, as in England, at least once every three years. To insure the election and meeting of the Assembly, the law provided that the first Commissioner should issue the writs, and if he failed, the next in commission. If no Commissioner acted, the sheriff should issue the writs, and if he failed, the county courts should assemble the people.[3] The name of Anne Arundel County was changed to Providence, and the land between it and St. Mary's was made Patuxent County.[4] St. Mary's name was shorn of the Saint, and authority was given to its inhabitants and to those of the Isle of Kent to set up county courts.[5]

---

was repealed, as were the laws concerning attachments and executions, deserted plantations, seating St. Inigoes fort, and mutinies and seditious speeches.

[1] 1 Md. Arch., Ass., 348; Bozman, II, 514.
[2] The records are to be kept at Mr. Richard Preston's, 1 Md. Arch., Ass., 347.
[3] 1 Md. Arch., Ass., 341, 345.
[4] 1 Md. Arch., Ass., 347.
[5] The secretary's and sheriff's fees are continued, 1 Md. Arch., Ass., 350, and Mr. Robert Brooke's petition for payment of his expenses is allowed, 354. The levy is given in detail, 355.

Taxes are to be laid as follows: a poll tax on every person, bond or free, negro, Indian, or European, except white women servants, and a tax of an aliquot part of the poll tax on each cow, horse, mule, or one hundred acres of land. The tenant for years shall not pay the land tax if the landlord lives in the county; but, if the landlord reside elsewhere, he shall pay the tax and may deduct it from his rent.[1] Registries of births, marriages, and deaths, and standards of weights and measures are to be kept by the clerk of the courts. The entrance and clearance of vessels are required.[2] Several of the laws deal with the aborigines, treating of war with Indians, stealing of friendly Indians, selling guns, powder, or shot to Indians, and the prohibition of Indians from trespassing on the settlers' lands, while a committee of nine residents of the Province was appointed to treat with Indians.[3]

The administration of estates,[4] the relation of servants and their masters,[5] the fugitive indentured servants,[6] a requirement that every taxable person planting tobacco plant also two acres of corn and place a strong fence four and one half feet high about the grain,[7] the offer of a reward for the killing of wolves,[8] the shutting out of foreigners from the Provincial trade,[9] the prohibition of engrossing and the regulation of accounts,[10] the ordering of the militia,[11] the striking of public officers,[12]—these are some of the subjects on which the Assembly legislated. The Puritanism of the members is seen in acts concerning drunkenness, swearing, theft, adultery and fornication, false reports,

---
[1] 1 Md. Arch., Ass., 342, 346.
[2] 1 Md. Arch., Ass., 345.
[3] 1 Md. Arch., Ass., 345, 346, 348, 349.
[4] 1 Md. Arch., Ass., 353, 354.
[5] 1 Md. Arch., Ass., 352.
[6] 1 Md. Arch., Ass., 348.
[7] 1 Md. Arch., Ass., 346, 349.
[8] 1 Md. Arch., Ass., 346.
[9] 1 Md. Arch., Ass., 351.
[10] 1 Md. Arch., Ass., 346, 351, 352.
[11] 1 Md. Arch., Ass., 347.
[12] 1 Md. Arch., Ass., 350.

slandering and talebearing, and the sanctity of the "Sabbath day;"[1] these acts, however, judged by the standard of the times, are not particularly severe.

IX. THE MARYLAND CIVIL WAR, 1654.

After the overthrow of the Proprietary government, the Puritans were anxious to justify themselves to the English people, and published in 1655 an answer to "The Lord Baltimore's Case," published two years previously, to which we have already referred. Like the pamphlet to which it is a reply, it is anonymous. It bears the name of "Virginia and Maryland, or The Lord Baltimore's [sic] printed Case Uncased and Answered."[2] It is a rather disordered work, written as soon as the news of the battle of the Severn reached England, and containing very valuable information as to events in 1654.

"Virginia and Maryland" was followed up by two other pamphlets written to justify the men of Providence, both

---

[1] 1 Md. Arch., Ass., 342-345. See Bozman, II, 513. John Sterman (3 Md. Arch., Coun., 313) petitioned the Assembly to have remitted a penalty imposed upon him and his father at Cornwallis's suit in the Provincial Court, because of the Stermans' acts in the time of Ingle's seizure of the Province, but the petition was not granted.

[2] Virginia and Maryland, or The Lord Baltimore's printed Case Uncased and Answered. Shewing, the illegality of his Patent and usurpation of Royal Jurisdiction and Dominion there. With, The Injustice and Tyranny practised in the Government, against the Laws and Liberties of the English Nation, and the just Right and Interest of the Adventurers and Planters. Also A short Relation of the Papists' late Rebellion against the Government of his Highness the Lord Protector, to which they were reduced by the Parliament's Commissioners; but since revolting, and by Lord Baltamore's instructions caused to assault the Protestants there in their Plantations, were by a far lesser number repulsed, some slain, and all the rest taken Prisoners. To which is added, A brief Account of the Commissioners' proceedings in the reducing of Maryland, with the Grounds and Reason thereof; the Commission and Instructions by which they acted; the Report of the Committee of the Navy, concerning that Province; and some other Papers and Passages relating thereunto; together with the Copy of a Writing under the Lord Baltamore's Hand and Seal, 1644, discovering his Practices, with the King at Oxford against the Parliament, concerning the Londoners and others trading in Virginia. 1655.

Reprinted in Force, Tracts and Other Papers, vol. II, no. 9, and in Hall, Narratives of Early Maryland, p. 181.

of which were issued in 1655. The former of these is written by Captain Roger Heamans of the *Golden Lion*, and is entitled " An Additional Brief Narrative of a late bloody design against the Protestants in Anne Arundel County."[1] It is worth noting that he describes the Province as " Maryland in the Country of Virginia." Though Heamans called himself " an eye witness," the Puritans were not content with his account as the official one, and another tract appeared, "published for Leonard Strong, agent for the people of Providence," and probably written by Strong. To this pamphlet the name was given of " Babylon's Fall in Maryland."[2] Heamans's work is almost entirely confined to the battle of the Severn and is the fullest account we have of the conflict. " Babylon's Fall " is an able and comprehensive review of the history of the Puritan party in Maryland from their first arrival in the Province during 1649, and contains an important narrative of the battle, but is a specious work, to be used with caution.

The two pamphlets issued by the Puritans gave rise to as many replies. John Hammond[3] had lived in Virginia for seventeen years, until 1652, when he sat in the Assembly as burgess from the Isle of Wight, and was expelled from the colony as " a scandalous person and a frequent disturber of the peace of the country," i. e., one opposed to the prevailing Puritan party. He went to Maryland, and now took on himself to reply to the " Additional Brief Nar-

---

[1] An Additional Brief *Narrative* of a late bloody design against the Protestants in Anne Arundel County Severn in Maryland in the Country of Virginia as also of the Extraordinary deliverance of those poor oppressed people Set forth by Roger Heamans, commander of the ship Golden Lyon—an eye witness there. 1655. Reprinted in Maryland Historical Magazine, IV, 140.

[2] Babylon's Fall in Maryland a fair Warning to Lord Baltamore or a Relation of an Assault made by divers Papists and Popish Officers of the Lord Baltamore's against the Protestants in Maryland; to whom God gave a great Victory against a greater force of Souldiers and armed Men, who came to destroy them. Published by Leonard Strong, Agent for the people of Providence in Maryland. Printed for the Author 1655. Reprinted in Maryland Historical Magazine, III, 228, and in Hall, 231.

[3] Neill, Terra Mariae, 127.

rative" in a partisan tract entitled "Hammond versus Heamans."[1]

The more official pamphlet, published by Strong, had a more official answer from "John Langford, Gentleman, servant to the Lord Baltimore," whom we have known as Surveyor in Maryland. Langford's tract is called "A Just and Cleere Refutation of a false and scandalous Pamphlet, Entituled Babylon's Fall in Maryland."[2] He states that for more than twenty years he has been acquainted with and employed by Baltimore, in Maryland and in England, on affairs concerning the Province. His work is a calm, dispassionate presentation of Baltimore's case down to July, 1654, especially defending the oath of fidelity. He prints the toleration act of 1649, intended "to prevent any disgusts between those of different judgments in religion," and defends both the reference to the Blessed Virgin Mary, by stating that "all Scripture calls her blessed," and the clause in the oath of officers allowing religious freedom to Roman Catholics, as a reasonable demand from Protestant officers by a Roman Catholic Proprietary. The Puritans are not

---

[1] Hammond versus Heamans Or An Answer To an audacious Pamphlet, published by an impudent and ridiculous Fellow, named Roger Heamans, Calling himself Commander of the Ship Golden Lion, wherein he endeavours by lies and holy expressions, to colour over his murthers and treacheries committed in the Province of Maryland, to the utter ruine of that florishing Plantation; Having for a great sum sold himself to proceed in those cruelties; it being altogether answered out of the abstract of credible oaths taken here in England. In which is published His Highness absolute (though neglected) Command to Richard Bennet, Esqr. late Governor of Va., and all others not to disturbe the Lord Baltamore's Plantation in Maryland. By John Hammond, a Sufferer in these Calamities. London, n. d.
This pamphlet is reprinted in Maryland Historical Magazine, IV, 236.

[2] A Just and Cleere Refutation of a false and scandalous Pamphlet, Entituled Babylon's Fall in Maryland &c and a true discovery of certaine strange and inhumane proceedings of some ungratefull people in Maryland toward those who formerly preserved them in time of their greatest distresse. To which is added a Law in Maryland concerning Religion, and a Declaration concerning the same. By John Langford, Gentleman, servant to the Lord Baltamore. London 1655.
This pamphlet is reprinted in Maryland Historical Magazine, IV, 42, and in Hall, 247.

contented with freedom for themselves of conscience, person, and estate, but wish the liberty to debar others of the like freedom, that they may domineer and do what they please. The bibliography of the conflict is completed by a second pamphlet from Hammond's pen entitled "Leah and Rachel, or the Two Fruitful Sisters; Virginia, and Mary-Land,"[1] in which he not only defends the Proprietary party in the past, but also endeavors to strengthen it by inviting new immigrants into the Province. He dedicates the pamphlet to James Williamson of Rappahannock and to Stone, "desirous that the whole country may note . . . that I dare in England own and entitle him my governor, that in Maryland I fled for submitting to." He tells us that for over two years he enjoyed life in Maryland, "but was enforced by reason of her unnatural disturbances to leave her weeping, . . . yet will I never wholly forsake or be beaten off from her." "Twice," he wrote, "hath she been deflowered by her own inhabitants, stript, shorn, & made deformed, yet such a natural fertility and comeliness doth she retain that she cannot but be loved, but be pitied." In his endeavor to attract settlers to the Province, he states that "it is (not an island as is reported) but is part of that main adjoining to Virginia, only separated or parted from Virginia by a river of 10 miles broad, called Potomac River, the commodities and manner of living as in Virginia, the soil somewhat more temperate, as being more northerly. Many stately and navigable rivers are contained in it, plentifully stored with wholesome springs, a rich and pleasant soil and so that its extraordinary goodness hath made it rather desired than envied, which hath been fatal to her (as beauty is often times to those that are endued with it)."

Moses Coit Tyler in his History of American Literature

---

[1] Leah and Rachel, or the Two Fruitful Sisters; Virginia and Mary-Land: Their present condition, Impartially stated and related with A Removal of such Imputations as are scandalously cast on those Countries, whereby many deceived Souls, chose rather to Beg, Steal, rot in Prison and come to shamefull deaths then to better their being by going thither, wherein is plenty of all things necessary for Humane subsistance. By John Hammond. London 1656. Reprinted in Force, vol. III, no. 14, and in Hall, 277.

calls this pamphlet " an extremely vigorous and sprightly tract," and speaks thus of its author: "He was a man of strong sense; he was very much in earnest; and he spoke his mind in a language so manly, frank, and vital, that even its uncouthness cannot take away the interest with which we stop and listen to him." Of "this clear headed and forceful American," Tyler further writes: "Here, thus early in our studies do we catch in American writings that new note of hope and of help for humanity in distress and of a rugged personal independence, which almost from the hour of our first settlements in this land, America began to send back, with unveiled exultation to Europe. . . . For the first time, perhaps, in the long experience of mankind on this planet, was then proclaimed this strong and jocund creed; and it was proclaimed first, as it has been since proclaimed continually in American literature."[1]

Hammond's reply to Heamans is characterized by heated invective. For example, he speaks of the Puritans as "inhuman, ungrateful, and blood sucking sectaries." He will answer the imbecility and villainy of Heamans, who is a "knave and a notorious offender." He had a "disordered ship," a "mutinous and quarrelsome company," who indulged in "drunken bouts and drawing of swords." In their insolency the seamen would sell commodities, and lighting on greater prices, repossessed themselves of the goods, scoffing at any pretence of law, and saying that their ship was of force enough to awe the whole country. They even robbed the planters' houses. Hammond tells us that he has written of the conditions under the tyranny of Bennett and Claiborne, but defers publishing this work.

From these five pamphlets we obtain practically all our knowledge of that battle which overthrew Baltimore's power and definitely wrested the Province from his hands for a time, and any narrative of these stirring events must needs be woven from the information they contain, with no help of importance from the Provincial records.

---

[1] I, 60-65.

The Maryland Civil War, 1654. 89

In November, 1654, Baltimore wrote Stone chiding him for his cowardice,[1] and told him that another governor would be appointed, unless he took vigorous action. About this time came also a vessel, commanded by Captain Samuel Tilghman, which bore a letter commending Dr. Luke Barber, written by Cromwell, in whose household Barber had been, and addressed to "Capt. Stone, Governor of Maryland." This title greatly encouraged the Proprietary party, as a manifest sign of the Protector's approval, so that, as the writer of "Virginia and Maryland" alleged, they "disarmed and plundered those that would not accept" the oath to the Proprietary. Eltonhead also came from England with news that Cromwell had neither taken Baltimore's patent from him nor his land, so that Stone now thought he might act by the contents of his former commission. Some of the Puritans stood on their guard and demanded of Stone that he show a commission from the Protector, before they would submit. He imprisoned their messengers, and with greater numbers assaulting them at their houses, abused them with opprobrious epithets.

The account given by the Proprietary author[2] is that, as Cromwell under his hand and signet had owned Stone's authority by addressing him as Governor, he endeavored to reassume the government, fetched away the records, proclaimed peace to all not obstinate, and favorably received many submissioners, who returned with a seeming joy. St. Mary's and Calvert Counties submitted. Anne Arundel and Kent must be subdued.

In the end of January there came to Maryland not only the ship *Golden Fortune,* Captain Samuel Tilghman, to which we have referred, but also the *Golden Lion,* Captain Roger Heamans, and these two vessels played an important part in the struggle. Tilghman was a warm supporter of the Proprietary cause, and when reproved by Captain John Smith, the Puritan sheriff, for addressing Stone as Governor, replied: "I must and shall own him and no other

---
[1] Virginia and Maryland; Bozman, II, 517 ff.; see 698.
[2] Hammond, Leah and Rachel.

for Governor of these parts. For, seeing my Lord Protector so styles him and by that title writes to him, I neither can nor dare call him otherwise and his example is my warrant." Smith brought news of this to Fuller, and they entered into treaty with Heamans and his ship, as Hammond alleges.[1]

Shortly after the arrival of the *Golden Fortune*, Stone sent Hammond unarmed with three or four oarsmen in a boat to Patuxent to take the Provincial records from Preston's house. While on that expedition, he saw a letter from Heamans to Preston, promising the use of his ship, ammunition, and men to the Puritans. This was the "first discovery" of danger to Stone, before he had a man in arms.[2] Hammond boasts that, unarmed, he later issued Stone's proclamation of pardon in Patuxent and put in office a new commander, in face of the whole county, who, as people overjoyed, acknowledged the Lord Proprietor as supreme lord and were pardoned.

The Puritans alleged that, when Hammond seized the records, threatening speeches were used, such as "We will have the government and hang, for the terror of others, some of the Commissioners." There were then sent from Providence two "messengers of quality and trust" to Stone, "in a way of peace and love," asking by what power he took the records.[3] Stone, in "much wrath and fury," said, "I will show no power—I acted by a power from the Lord Baltimore and the Lord Protector confirmed Baltimore's power." "If so, sir," said one of the messengers, "if it be confirmed, let that appear and it will satisfy." "Confirmed," said Stone, "I'll confirm it," and sent the messenger home.

After Hammond proclaimed Stone's intention "to use no

---
[1] Hammond, Hammond versus Heamans.
[2] In Leah and Rachel, Hammond claims that Heamans had, Judas-like, promised to be instrumental to the Governor, and that his perfidy was found out only at the time of the battle. Hammond is not fully trustworthy. Barber says that the Puritans hired Heamans and paid him.
[3] Strong, Babylon's Fall.

hostile way," the latter sent twenty men in arms, under Eltonhead and Fendall, who beset and entered Preston's house, to surprise him, as the Puritans said, or more probably to search for arms. He was away, so they ransacked the house, taking therefrom guns, swords, and ammunition. They carried away also John Sutton,[1] who had been appointed by the Assembly "to attend the Records for any that should have occasion to use them, either for search or copy." They also searched Lieutenant Peter Johnson's and other houses, and when asked by what power they so acted, they clapped their hands on their swords and said, "Here is a commission."

On March 5 from Providence there was sent a "dignified, sober missive "[2] to Stone, signed by Fuller, Durand, Preston, Strong, and Ewing, asking why he seized the records, and requiring him, in the name of Cromwell, that for the peace and welfare of the Province he make known to them and the free inhabitants of the Province, in an orderly and legal way, if he had any "higher power than is here established by the Commissioners of the Commonwealth." The Puritan leaders stated that they "affect not preëminence, but had much rather be governed ourselves by the laws of God and lawful authority of him set over us, than that we ourselves should be in an employment the nature whereof in these times is above our abilities and those that are far more able." They adjure him to take "care that the country be not brought to ruin and desolation, whilst you think to heal the breaches thereof." The letter is so finely expressed and of such excellent temper that we cannot but feel that Baltimore was badly served by Stone in not giving courteous answer. In fact, Stone was in a difficult position, and he seems not to have shown much tact or skill in managing the difficulties which surrounded him. The request that he show his right to take up the governorship, after resigning the office in the preceding summer, was on the face of it a

---
[1] He was kept prisoner for twenty days.
[2] Printed in Heamans, An Additional Brief Narrative.

reasonable one, and to show the superscription of a letter was hardly a satisfactory reply to the request.

In March, Stone sent Henry Coursey and Luke Barber to Anne Arundel with a proclamation[1] summoning the people to yield obedience to Baltimore's officers under the Lord Protector. The people were found in arms, and Fuller would not permit Coursey to read the proclamation, which contained a statement that Stone wished to reclaim them by fair means. He dismissed the envoys, but before they could get away, ordered them held as prisoners, so that Stone received no reply. He forthwith marched against the Puritans with his men, commanding them under pain of death to do no plunder and not to fire the first gun if they met any of the Anne Arundel men.

Let us now hear what Captain Heamans tells of his movements.[2] He first anchored the *Golden Lion* in the Patuxent. While in that river, on January 31 a boat containing Stone and about four other persons came to the vessel. Heamans called the company to man the ship's side to accommodate Stone's coming on board, after which Heamans called for wine and drank to him as Governor Stone. This may have been before Stone saw the Protector's letter, so Heamans may have written truly that Stone said: "I have formerly been governor, but am not so now. The governor at present is one Capt. Fuller, a gentleman lately settled by the Commissioners of Parliament and now at Severn."[3] Heamans said that he heard nothing of any difference or hostile preparation[4] while there, and on February

---

[1] Hammond, Hammond versus Heamans. Strong, in Babylon's Fall, says that they were permitted to read the proclamation and then were dismissed, and places the embassy just before the battle, after Stone's march. Bozman (II, 520) calls attention to the fitness of Barber for the embassy, as a neutral person and one in the confidence of the Protector. Langford, A Just and Cleere Refutation.
[2] Heamans, An Additional Brief Narrative.
[3] Hammond, in Hammond versus Heamans, quibbles that Stone could not have said this, as Fuller was only one of the Commissioners. True, but popularly he was doubtless known as Governor.
[4] Hammond denies Heamans's statement as to his lack of knowledge of any difference, saying that on Heamans's ship and in Hammond's hearing Stone and Hatton had words with Preston, complaining of

15 set sail for Severn, where he arrived late at night. The next morning he went ashore and paid his respects to Fuller. Heamans continued trading there for a month, when he left the ship in the hands of his mate and went to Rhode River, "7 leagues distant," to procure goods. He was soon recalled by a message from Fuller, requiring him "presently" to attend him and with his men to repair to the ship. As he approached the *Golden Lion* he heard the firing of a piece of her ordnance, and when he came on board, found Fuller there and was told that the firing was by his orders. Fuller then said to Heamans: "I have received certain intelligence that Stone, with a party of Roman Catholics, malignants and disaffected persons, who had called to their assistance a great number of heathen, were in arms and that they forced along with them what others they could not by favor persuade, plundering all that refuse to assist them. They privately design the destruction of the Governor and all the Protestants of Severn and to destroy men, women, and children that shall not submit to their wicked design. This is under pretence of bringing into subjection to the Lord Proprietary us, whom they call those factious people in the county of Anne Arundel. They do not own, in the least, the Lord Protector's power. The design is also against you and your ship and company, if they will not assist Stone, to fire your ship while riding anchor. This is to be effected by Abraham Hely,[1] a seaman who ran away from the *Golden Lion* at Patuxent. This design is so settled that Stone and his soldiery are ready to march. The sudden news of such horrid treachery has put the poor inhabitants in a lamentable condition, former experience having shown them the malice of their adversaries against all that own the way of God in truth. May the trembling women and children come on board your ship?"

---

the Puritans' "injurious assuming of government" and taking of the records, and threatening that, unless they returned them again, the Proprietary party would compel them to go away (ibid.).

[1] Hammond says that Hely is of "honest temper" and ran away on account of Heamans's "fantastic domineerings" (ibid.).

94   *Maryland Under the Commonwealth.*

Whether Heamans has exaggerated Fuller's speech, or whether the latter himself exaggerated conditions wilfully, or was so terrified as to lose his head, we know not. Heamans at once granted Fuller's request, and then the Commissioners drafted a letter which was signed by Durand and sent Stone, in the ship's wherry, demanding his power and the ground of his proceeding, and proposing to yield to him if he would govern them " so as we may enjoy the liberties of English subjects," allow them to " remain indemnified in respects of our engagements and all former acts relating to the reducement of government, and permit those minded to depart the Province to do so, without any prejudice to themselves or their estate." If Stone will not grant these terms, the Puritans " are resolved to commit themselves into the hands of God and rather die like men than be made slaves."

At the Cliffs the wherry met Stone with his men, some marching by land and others proceeding in sloops and boats. In a rage Stone took away the wherry and commanded the messengers to be taken into guard. Two[1] of them escaped, however, came to Severn, and told Fuller what had occurred. The latter thereupon, on March 22, wrote to Heamans commanding him, with ship and men, to be " for the service of the Lord Protector and Commonwealth of England, in assisting to your power the people of Providence " against Baltimore's men. On the next day Fuller directed Heamans to seize and detain any vessels arriving there to disturb the government here settled. By Fuller's commands, these orders were affixed to the mast of the *Golden Lion* and Heamans agreed to obey them. Stone had mustered two hundred or two hundred and fifty men in arms at Eltonhead's house, and Eltonhead and Fendall sent up by night several boats with armed men to Patuxent, where they forced many to go with them, took all the guns, ammunition, and provision they could find, and are said to have done some plundering.[2] At Herring Creek the advancing forces

---
[1] Strong, in Babylon's Fall, says that three escaped.
[2] Strong, Babylon's Fall.

apprehended a Commissioner and forced another man of quality to fly for his life, threatening to hang him up at his own door. Not finding him at home, they frightened his wife and took what ammunition and provisions they could find.[1]

On the evening of the twenty-third a boat came to the *Golden Lion* bearing a messenger and a letter from Stone to Heamans, desiring him not to assist the people of Severn against Baltimore's government.[2] Heamans took the letter ashore to Fuller and his council, who told him that it was of no great weight, and that he should answer it as he thought best and send away the messenger. Heamans replied, stating that at Patuxent Stone had disclaimed authority from the Protector and must now show it in order to have Heamans's service.[3] Unless he sees such authority, Heamans will obey "the government settled on Capt. Fuller by the supreme power of England and since established by the Lord Protector." One Richard Owen, a merchant aboard the *Golden Lion,* wrote to Stone defending Heamans's position, urging that Stone show any commission he might have from Cromwell, and signing himself "your friend and kinsman."

Heamans now had received most of his freight on board the *Golden Lion,* and on the morning of March 24 went ashore to tell Fuller that, "in pursuance of his employers trust, he intended to get his water aboard and so depart the port." Fuller and his Commissioners, knowing that Stone's army was near at hand, sent an especial warrant for Heamans and gave him strict charge, in the Protector's name, not to depart without Fuller's order. This document, while Heamans was ashore, was sent on board the *Golden Lion* and nailed to the mast. On his return to the ship,

---

[1] Strong, in Babylon's Fall, states that the women, bereft of arms and men, feared lest the Indians should attack them, and that the Indians beset houses after the fight, killed two men, and took some prisoners.
[2] Hammond, in Hammond versus Heamans, gives the alleged letter.
[3] Heamans, in An Additional Brief Narrative, gives text of Heamans's reply. He showed Stone's messenger Fuller's orders.

Heamans, whose sympathies were warmly with the Puritans, debated with his officers and company, and found them unanimously of the opinion that they ought to "relieve those poor distressed people." Therefore, he resolved not to leave the port till "God put an end to the restless condition of their brethren and suffered their deliverance to be wrought." That afternoon Heamans again went ashore to have his bills of lading prepared, and he was told that the enemy was entering the mouth of the harbor with a great number of sloops and boats full of armed men, with drums and colors. He was directed to return to the ship with two of the Commissioners and there to obey their orders.

"In the very shutting up of the daylight,"[1] on March 24, a company of sloops and boats was descried making toward the *Golden Lion,* whereupon the Commissioners on board and the crew would have "made shot" at them; but Heamans commanded the men to forbear, and going to the poop in the stern, hailed the boats several times. No answer was made, and he then charged them not to come nearer the ship. They kept on rowing, and were come within shot of the ship when his mates and the company, having had information of the threatenings of Stone's men, resolved to fire without Heamans's consent, rather than hazard all. He then ordered them to fire a gun at random to divert the course of Stone's fleet, which was done, but the latter "kept course with the ship," and took no notice of the warning. Heamans then commanded that the ordnance should be fired at the boats.

Another shot was fired, aimed near the boats,[2] and a messenger came toward the *Golden Lion* to say that Stone thought Heamans had been satisfied. To this Heamans replied: "Satisfied with what? I never saw any power Capt. Stone had, to do as he hath done, but the superscription of

---

[1] Strong, in Babylon's Fall, says that Fuller told Heamans to command them aboard by ordnance, but Stone's forces with great noise rejected the warning.

[2] Strong, Babylon's Fall. Hammond, in Leah and Rachel, says that the messengers were retained. Heamans, in An Additional Brief Narrative, does not speak of them.

The Maryland Civil War, 1654.

a letter. I must and will appear for these men in a good cause." Shortly afterwards the men in the boats altered their course and rowed toward the creek, calling the ship's company "rogues, roundheads, dogs," and threatening to fire the vessel in the morning. The boats ran into the creek now known as Spa or Acton Creek that night, and landed out of reach of the ship.[1] In the morning Fuller ordered a small vessel, with two pieces of ordnance, commanded by Captain Cutts of New England, to lie in the mouth of the creek and so keep the enemy's craft from coming out.

At daybreak on the morning of Sunday, March 25, the anniversary of Leonard Calvert's first landing in Maryland, Stone and his whole body of about two hundred men[2] appeared, drawn out and coming toward the waterside, marching with drums beating and the black and yellow colors flying, as Baltimore had appointed. Heamans noted that there was no token of subjection to the Protector Cromwell in the Proprietary army. Heamans then fired at them, killed one of their number, and forced them to march further off into the neck of land. When Fuller saw Stone's forces, "after earnest seeking of God and laying" the Puritans' "innocence at His feet," he resolved, with "humble cheerfulness, to go over to the enemy." So he sent to the *Golden Lion* for the ship's English colors, and fixing them to a half pike, he went over the river some six miles distant from the enemy, leading something over one hundred men from Anne Arundel and Kent, rather more than half of Stone's force, without music, for he had no drum. He probably went from Greenberry Point by boat across the Severn, then landing, he marched around the head of Spa Creek to the present Horn Point, if Bozman and J. W. Randall are right as to the site of the battle.[3] Arriving at

---
[1] Chalmers (An Introduction to the History of the Revolt of the American Colonies, I, 80) says that Heamans's treachery compelled Stone to land on a narrow neck.
[2] Puritans say two hundred and fifty, Hammond, in Leah and Rachel, says one hundred and thirty.
[3] Hammond, in Leah and Rachel, says that one hundred and seventy men were with Fuller. D. R. Randall (A Puritan Colony,

an open place near where Stone and his men stood, Fuller pitched his colors, for he thought that the Proprietary forces might come to a parley and prevent bloodshed when they saw the standard of the Commonwealth. But Stone's sentry fired the alarm gun, the army appeared in order, and made several shots at the setting down of the colors, killing two of Fuller's men.[1] Then Fuller gave the word, "In the name of God fall on, God is our strength," and with it he gave fire. The Governor's men were on a neck of land, with the *Golden Lion* on one side and the Anne Arundel men coming in upon them from the other, thus cutting off retreat.

It was the feast of the Virgin Mary, and Stone's company, largely from St. Mary's, engaged with great boldness, shouting, "Hey for St. Mary's," to which one narrator adds, "Hey for our wives." Some of the rougher fellows are said to have changed the latter cry to "Hey for two wives," as if they expected the rape of women should follow upon victory, as it had so recently in the battles of the German Thirty Years' War. The dispute was short but sharp, and with true Puritan reference to Old Testament language, the Providence men said that in their victory "God confounded Capt. Stone and his company before us." The Proprietary army "gave back and were so effectually charged home that they were all routed, turned their backs, threw down their arms, and begged mercy." A small company of Stone's men, after the first volley from "behind a fallen tree, galled Fuller and wounded divers of his men," but were soon beaten off. Thomas Hatton, the Secretary, and over twenty of the Proprietary army were slain;[2] many were wounded, among them Stone, who was shot in the shoulder and in "many places," and many were taken prisoners, leaving the "ground strewed with papist beads."[3] Hammond

---

39) says that the battle field was the present site of Annapolis. Another view, held by J. W. Randall (14) and Bozman (II, 523), places the battle field on Horn Point.
[1] Strong, in Babylon's Fall, says that one was killed.
[2] Heamans says that forty were slain.
[3] Virginia and Maryland.

maintains that Stone yielded on being promised quarter, but being in hold was threatened with immediate death unless he would write to the rest to take quarter, which they did upon his request. The victory seemed, to Heamans and to the Puritans, an "unparalleled mercy." Notwithstanding the thickness of the woods, only four or five of Stone's followers finally escaped from the place which the exultant victors called the " Papish pound," as if the vanquished had been impounded there, while only three of Fuller's men were killed on the field and three others afterwards died of their wounds.[1] The Puritans had right to hold a " religious, humble and holy rejoicing." They had taken "all the arms bag and baggage," the boats and their stores, the pictures, crucifixes, and a great store of relics. In his despondency Stone said that he was cursed, and according to Heamans, took the defeat as a judgment upon him for his alliance with the Roman Catholics. Heamans said that, when he came ashore after the fight, the prisoners were in such fear that they durst not run away, though the poor tired people slept who were keeping the door of the house used as a prison.

After the surrender,[2] Stone and most of the prisoners were transported over the river to the fort, where they were kept prisoners for three days. Then a council of war was assembled with the membership of Fuller, William Burgess,[3] Richard Ewens, Leonard Strong, Durand, Heamans, John Brown, John Cutts, Richard Smith, Thomas Thomas, Thomas Bestone, Samson Warren or Waring, Thomas Meares, and Ralph Crouch, and this council condemned to death practically all of the Proprietary Councilors and several of the lesser men of Baltimore's party, namely, Stone, Colonel John Price, Major Job Chandler, William Eltonhead,[4] Robert Clarke, Captain Nicholas Gwyther, Wil-

---

[1] Strong, in Babylon's Fall, says that two died of wounds and two were killed.
[2] Hammond, Hammond versus Heamans.
[3] Davis, 70.
[4] Neill (Virginia Carolorum, 121, 254, 410, 421) says that Elton-

liam Evans, Captain William Lewis, John Leggat, and John Pedro, "a German which did live with Mr. Eltonhead." At the request of the soldiers and of the women several were spared, some being saved as they were being led out to execution, but the Puritans' victory was sullied by the execution of Eltonhead, Lewis, Leggat, and Pedro. Eltonhead asked that he be allowed to appeal to Cromwell, but this was denied him. Why these four men were selected for execution we do not know. Fendall was also among those tried,[1] as was Hely, who "confessed that he was solicited by divers eminent officers" under Stone to set fire to or blow up the *Golden Lion,* for which service he should receive twenty thousand pounds of tobacco. Heamans then returned to England, stopping at Patuxent, where Hely ran away again. Leonard Strong probably went to England with Heamans, to publish the vindication of the Puritans' acts, and shortly afterwards died in his mother-country. Captain Tilghman, with the *Golden Fortune,* sailed in April, bringing with him to England a piteous letter to Baltimore from Virlinda Stone, Governor Stone's wife, who had not seen her husband since the battle, and an indignant one from Barber to the Lord Protector, in which he begged Cromwell to "condescend so low as to settle this country."[2] Hammond tells us that he was proscribed to die by the Puritans,[3] fled disguised to Virginia, and was brought to England in the ship *Crescent,* Captain Thorowgood, because of which service the dominant party amerced the captain for bringing away Virginians without a pass, though Hammond was a Marylander and not a Virginian.[4]

After the executions the common soldiers in Stone's army were sent away, but the officers and messengers were kept

---

head was a brother-in-law of Henry Corbyn, and that he probably married Jane, widow of Philip Taylor, who had been with Smith in the Pocomoke naval battle.

[1] Heamans, An Additional Brief Narrative.
[2] Bozman, II, 687.
[3] Hammond, in Hammond versus Heamans, says that Dr. Barber was imprisoned, fined, and nearly executed.
[4] Hammond, Leah and Rachel.

longer, and Coursey and Gwyther had imposed on them by the council of war an oath not to write to Baltimore about the matter.[1] The Puritan Commissioners followed with amercements and sequestrations of the property of some of the leading members of the Proprietary party, some of which we shall come upon in the proceedings of the Provincial Court, and the Province passed entirely out of the hands of Baltimore's officers for three years.

X. Conditions after the War.

On April 24, 1655, Captain Robert Sly was made by the Commissioners one of their body, to act as a full Councilor, but especially to see to the "administration of justice and government in the limits of St. Mary's and Potomac." With Sly, John Hatch and John Lawson were appointed to issue writs for the courts, and the two latter should also assist Sly in "repelling and suppressing any opposition against the present government, made by the Lord Baltimore or any other."[2] At the same time Captains John Smith and Peter Johnson were appointed as commanders of the military forces on both sides of Patuxent River, and Captain Smith was also appointed to take care of the sequestered estates of delinquents and to be muster master general for St. Mary's, Potomac, and Patuxent Counties.[3] Captain Sampson Waring was appointed commander of the forces residing on Herring Creek, and Captains John Sly and Richard Hodgkeys were appointed to command the militia in St. Mary's and Potomac River. Captain John Sly was appointed President of the St. Mary's County court, and six Commissioners were named with him, three of whom were of the quorum. The same number of Commissioners was appointed for Patuxent County court, and it was ordered that the jurisdiction of these courts should be limited to three thousand pounds of tobacco and £20 sterling and to such criminal actions "as

[1] Hammond, Hammond versus Heamans.
[2] 3 Md. Arch., Coun., 315.
[3] 3 Md. Arch., Coun., 315; 10 Md. Arch., Prov. Ct., 412, 413, 417.

extend not to life or member."[1] This organization was the result of the "late war raised by Capt. Stone and his complices," as the court styled it, and that war caused them much concern. William Evans, "convicted of high offence against the public," humbly acknowledged his offence, and was granted mercy, upon paying two thousand pounds of tobacco and cask "towards the public damage" caused by that war.[2] John Ashcombe claimed that he was in drink and "some way submitted to" Stone and his party, "through fear of mischief threatened by them," and was fined the same amount.[3] "The petitioners of Patuxent" were discharged, "by an act of favor past unto them," from all damage arising from their petition, doubtless against the Puritan regime, as they made "acknowledgment of their offence and free submission to the present government." Richard Collett had subscribed a "petition of dangerous contents," and so was "convicted of a scandalous offence against the government," and was banished from the Province. He must pay one thousand pounds of tobacco; but, if he should give sufficient security, he might remain until Christmas and settle his affairs as manager of a Virginian's plantation in Maryland.

Lieutenant Richard Banks and Thomas Tunnell, who had been in arms with Stone, cravenly pleaded that "they were misled by the protestation of Capt. Stone, who said he had power from the Lord Protector," pointed out that they "did surrender a fort upon the first summons," and were discharged "upon their submission."[4] In October, Banks was again summoned before the court and made to furnish security for his "good abearance to the public government and to all the people thereof," as he had "again done something to obstruct the choice of the Burgesses."

John Metcalf, the sheriff, had pressed a man's boat, by "Capt. Stone's appointment," in the "last insurrection," and

---

[1] 10 Md. Arch., Prov. Ct., 413.
[2] 10 Md. Arch., Prov. Ct., 413.
[3] 10 Md. Arch., Prov. Ct., 414.
[4] 10 Md. Arch., Prov. Ct., 414.

Conditions After the War. 103

he was ordered to satisfy the man therefor.[1] The same man also complained that "he had several goods taken from him, when the soldier was last at Maryland," and he was authorized to have "examined by some magistrate three or four of that company, which he hath in suspicion."[2]

On May 21 a court met at Providence under "Capt. General" Fuller's presidency, and ordered, in accordance with the Act of Assembly, that Hatton, late Secretary, should have power of distress for the fees "due to him before the resignation of the Government by Capt. William Stone, July, 1654."[3]

Of the clergy in the colony we learn little during the Commonwealth. Father Copley died in 1652, and his successor, Father Lawrence Starkey,[4] who was born in 1606 and joined the Jesuits in 1636, died on February 19, 1657. In 1654 Father Francis Fitzherbert came, and wrote home of sickness on the vessel during the voyage, of the terrible storm which they experienced, causing the mariners to slay a little old woman suspected by them of sorcery, and of how all hands worked at the pumps to save the vessel.

After the battle of the Severn the Jesuits' houses were plundered and the fathers fled secretly to Virginia.[5] They had escaped "grievous dangers" and "great difficulties and straits," but they lived there in "a mean hut, low and depressed, not much unlike a cistern, having lost the stipend which they had expected from England," as the ship bearing it had been intercepted. They had not enough wine for the sacrament of the eucharist, and no servant, not even one to steer or row their boat. "Often over spacious and vast

---

[1] 10 Md. Arch., Prov. Ct., 416.
[2] 10 Md. Arch., Prov. Ct., 418.
[3] 10 Md. Arch., Prov. Ct., 549; Bozman, II, 525. Hatton was slain in the battle, and the vote was for his widow's benefit, 3 Md. Arch., Coun., 325.
[4] Neill, Founders of Maryland, 127; Shea, The Catholic Church in Colonial Days, 75; "Relatio Itineris in Marylandiam," Maryland Historical Society, Fund Publication no. 7, p. 90.
[5] "Relatio Itineris in Marylandiam," Maryland Historical Society, Fund Publication no. 7, p. 91. They reported that three of the four men shot in the battle were Roman Catholics.

rivers, one of them, alone and unaccompanied, passes and repasses long distances, with no other pilot directing his course than Divine Providence."

In 1650 there came to the Province one William Wilkinson, a clergyman of the Anglican church, a man about fifty years old, with his wife, three daughters, a stepdaughter, and two servants.[1] He engaged in trade to support his family.

We hear not much of Kent Island during these years. The county records show that as early as 1652 John Winchester was taking up land there with an agreement to plant it with apple, cherry, pear, and peach trees. This proof of the early fruit culture is confirmed by an affidavit made by John Dobb in 1653 that Thomas Lombard gave over an estate to Thomas Marsh in cherry time. In this latter year Hatton sent John Coursey or DeCourcy,[2] the first of his well-known line, to the island with a letter of introduction, and in 1655 we find that Thomas Hawkins sold a tract known as Westmoreland, comprising half of Popley's Island, and that William Leeds sold fifty acres cleared for seven thousand tobacco plants, a culture now abandoned in great part on the Eastern Shore.

Stone was not satisfied to submit to his overthrow, and sent[3] one William Watson a warrant to publish a proclamation and to read to the people and tender them for their signature a letter of submission to his government. There were other evidences that the Proprietary party was not dead. Thomas Arley, or Orley, about the close of September,[4] refused to give Henry Potter an assurance for property which Potter bought of Edward Hall, whose ad-

---

[1] Neill, Terra Mariae, 123, Founders of Maryland, 124. One daughter married Wm. Hatton and another Thos. Dent, both Protestants. Dent lived within the limits of the present District of Columbia. In 1672 Rev. Mr. Nicolet, of Salem, Mass., who had lived in Maryland, spoke of knowing five Protestants there, viz., Messrs. Dent, Hatton, Hill, Hanson, and Thorowgood.

See Davis, 153, for some questionable acts of Rev. Mr. Wilkinson.
[2] Davis, 114, 201.
[3] 10 Md. Arch., Prov. Ct., 434.
[4] 10 Md. Arch., Prov. Ct., 434, 438, 453.

ministrator Orley was, as "there is no law nor Government in Maryland." Potter's wife replied, "There is both law and government, if we will go to Patuxent for it," to which Orley answered: "Patuxent men do not grant true justice and, for Fuller, he durst not call a court. The Governor of Virginia sent order to the contrary and will order him for what he had done already." Orley seems formerly to have lived on the land sold, and by his lease was bound to leave housing and fencing tenantable.[1]

Though Baltimore's commission to Fendall to act as Governor of the Province was not signed until the summer of 1656, he had been openly acting "to the disturbance of the public peace" by assuming a power from Stone, though he had taken an oath to the "present government."[2] Fendall was charged with this, and did not satisfactorily traverse the charge, but "rather disowned the power of the Court." As he gave "just ground of suspicion of his dangerousness to the public peace of this Province" if he should enjoy his liberty, he was ordered to go "to the place from whence he came a prisoner and there abide in safe custody, until the matters of government in the Province of Maryland shall be further settled" by the English authorities, to which decree Fendall consented. Almost a year later, on September 24, 1656, he took oath in open court that he would not be "a disturber to this present government, till there be a full determination ended in England of all matters relating to this Government."[3]

Cromwell wrote to Bennett[4] from Whitehall on January 12, 1654/5, upbraiding him because, although the "differences between the Lord Baltimore and the inhabitants of Virginia, concerning the bounds by them respectively claimed," were as yet undecided by the Privy Council, Ben-

---
[1] 10 Md. Arch., Prov. Ct., 460, 467 (464, 469, 470, a jury trial in October, 1656, in which Orley won), 477.
[2] 10 Md. Arch., Prov. Ct., 427, 463.
[3] 10 Md. Arch., Prov. Ct., 463.
[4] Carlyle, Oliver Cromwell's Letters and Speeches, IV, 74; Andrews and Davenport, Guide to the Manuscript Material for the History of the United States to 1783, in the British Museum, 381; Rawlinson Ms. 43. f. 101.

106   Maryland Under the Commonwealth.

nett had "gone into" Maryland and "countenanced some people there in opposing the Lord Baltimore's officers; whereby and with other forces from Virginia" Bennett had "much disturbed that Colony and people, to the endangering of tumults and much bloodshed there, if not timely prevented." Of this conduct Baltimore complained, as did "divers other persons of quality" in England, "who are engaged by great adventures in his interest," so Cromwell commanded Bennett and "all others deriving any authority from you" not to disturb "Baltimore, or his officers or people, in Maryland and to permit all things to remain as they were, before any disturbance or alteration made by you or by any other, upon pretence of authority from you; till the said differences above mentioned be determined by us here and we give further order therein." Bennett thereupon made further representations to Cromwell, and the Maryland Commissioners also wrote[1] Cromwell on June 29 giving their side of the case; so from Whitehall, on September 26, 1655, Cromwell wrote to the Commissioners of Maryland[2] that a mistake had arisen concerning the January letter, which was being interpreted as directing that a stop be "put to the proceedings of those Commissioners who were authorized to settle the civil government of Maryland." Cromwell wrote that this "was not at all intended, nor indeed asked by Baltimore and his friends," but Cromwell wished to "prevent and forbid any force or violence to be offered" by either Virginia or Maryland to the other "upon the differences concerning their bounds," which differences were being considered by the Privy Council.

XI. Josias Fendall, Governor, 1656.

A year later Baltimore thought that the time had come for him to act, and on July 10, 1656, he appointed Josias Fendall Governor of the Province in place of Stone, to the end that there might be good government established, "for the

---
[1] Carlyle, IV, 133.
[2] Bozman, II, 532. Bennett had gone to England.

Josias Fendall, Governor, 1656. 107

cherishing and supporting of the good people and well affected, as for the punishment of the vicious and disorderly persons."[1] The Proprietary probably felt that Stone's administration had aroused many animosities and that a new Governor would more easily reestablish harmony in Maryland. Stone was retained, however, as first Councilor and there were also appointed to the Council Thomas Gerard, Colonel John Price, Job Chandler, Luke Barber, and others, not exceeding three in number, to be named by Fendall, who was likewise authorized to name a Secretary and receiver general. Fendall had commanded the party sent by Stone to seize arms and ammunition at the Patuxent, and had been in the battle of March 26 as one of the Proprietary's soldiers. These and doubtless other forgotten proofs of zeal in the cause induced Baltimore to confide to him the government of the Province.

The Proprietary, under date of October 23, sent instructions to Fendall,[2] from which we learn interesting facts concerning the controversy in England. After Baltimore's complaint to the Protector, in 1655, that he "was interrupted in his rights and jurisdictions in Maryland," Cromwell, on November 2, appointed Bulstrode Whitlock and Sir Thomas Widdrington to examine into the matter. They reported on May 26, 1656, but their report is unfortunately lost. It must have been favorable to Baltimore, however, for on petition of Bennett and Samuel Matthews, as "agents for Virginia and the rest of the Plantations in the Bay of Chesapeake," the report and its accompanying papers were referred to the Committee for Trade[3] on July 31. This last body asked Bennett and Matthews "to make some proposals for the settlement and peace" of Maryland.

---

[1] 3 Md. Arch., Coun., 323; Bozman, II, 534. McMahon (An Historical View of the Government of Maryland from its Colonization to the Present Day, 210) says of Fendall that "his treachery is conspicuous in almost every transaction with which he is connected." He was untrue to his compact with the Commissioners and to his commission from Baltimore.
[2] Bozman, II, 537; 3 Md. Arch., Coun., 324.
[3] Thurloe, A Collection of the State Papers of John Thurloe, 482; Bozman, II, 470, 540, 690.

These proposals were received and also some answers from Baltimore, with which answers Bennett and Matthews declared themselves satisfied. On September 16 the committee made its report to Cromwell, which seems to have favored Baltimore. There was still delay from some unknown cause, and on December 17 the Council of State referred the whole matter to the Committee for Foreign Plantations.[1] A month later nothing had been done. Bozman[2] is probably correct in his sage surmise that the claim of Virginia for the whole of Maryland had been rejected by the Protector in 1655, and that only the disputes "that had happened between the men of Severn and Lord Baltimore's officers" were under further consideration.

Baltimore's instructions to Fendall of October, 1656, were written while he was still uncertain of the final outcome in England,[3] but was encouraged to believe that his claims would be successful. He directed his lieutenant that, when the people who opposed his government should have quietly and peacefully submitted themselves, the act concerning religion of 1649 should be again enforced. A new great seal would soon be sent. Two thousand acres of land were to be set out to Fendall, as had been promised him by a letter of August 23, and one thousand acres each to five others of the Proprietary's followers.[4] Mrs. Hatton, Mrs. Lewis, and Mrs. Eltonhead, the widows of the men shot by the Puritans, were to be supplied out of the Proprietor's rents in case they were in need, and they were to be assured that Baltimore "will continue his utmost endeavors, by soliciting" Cromwell and his Council, to procure them justice for their husbands' deaths and satisfaction for their losses.

[1] 3 Md. Arch., Coun., 330, see 332. In August, 1657, proposals for transporting Irish to Maryland from England were respited by the Council of State. Virginia Magazine of History and Biography, XVIII, 152.
[2] II, 538.
[3] 3 Md. Arch., Coun., 325.
[4] Luke Barber, Thomas Trueman, George Thomson, John Langford, and Henry Coursey. Barber and Trueman had been promised also in August. Quit rents of a shilling for fifty acres were reserved on the lands.

Baltimore also directed Fendall to tell them to let Baltimore "know wherein he can do them any good" in Maryland, "in recompense of their sufferings, of which he is very sensible." Further paragraphs[1] in the instructions directed that persons who have been faithful and "done good service in the late troubles" should be "cherished and comforted" and preferred to places of trust and profit,[2] and that Baltimore be informed "wherein he can upon any occasion requite them." The Council must take care to prevent encroachments from being made upon the Province, especially on the side of Virginia, which colony had recently claimed the whole of Maryland.[3] It is quite probable, as Bozman surmises, that Baltimore prepared these instructions to his Council in "exact conformity to the report of the commissioners for trade."[4]

A month later the Proprietary issued new instructions to his Governor and Council and sent them over by his brother, Philip Calvert, whom he commissioned as a Councilor and as Secretary of the Province. Calvert was directed to administer the oath of office to Fendall and to have laid out for him six thousand acres of land, to be erected into one or more manors.[5] Additional grants of one hundred and of two hundred acres were made to two men,[6] and fifty acres were promised to every servant "that hath and shall serve out his time with any planter" and "approve himself faithful" to Baltimore. Greater caution in these new grants was shown, in that the stretch of the grant along the water was limited to fifty poles in every fifty acres.[7] These November instructions also directed all sheriffs and coroners to give bond before they entered their offices.

[1] Gibbons's windmill at St. Mary's had been assigned by his widow to Baltimore, and the Proprietary directed the Council to care for it.
[2] Thomas Trueman, George Thomson, Lieutenant Thomas Tunnell, and William Barton are especially mentioned.
[3] Lost maps of the two Provinces are referred to.
[4] Bozman, II, 543.
[5] 3 Md. Arch., Coun., 329 (November 12); Bozman, II, 545. Philip Calvert was to perform the functions of land commissioner and of register of wills.
[6] William Thomson and Paul Simpson.
[7] All this land paid the usual quit rent.

Philip Calvert had arrived in the Province before June 8, 1657, when he and Fendall held a Council at St. Mary's and the latter, nominated Luke Barber to be his deputy[1] while he was out of the Province on a voyage to England. This absence lasted until February 26, 1657/8, but Barber's tenure of office was probably only nominal, as the actual rule of the Province was in the hands of the Commissioners.[2]

The second and last of the Assemblies held under the authority of Fuller and the other Commissioners met at Patuxent, probably at Mr. Preston's house, on September 24, 1657.[3] We have no knowledge how it was summoned, or what part was taken by the various members. Eleven of the Commissioners assembled as the Provincial[4] Court on the twenty-second under Preston's presidency, and that court sat daily, except Sunday, until October 1 and again on October 5. We do not know how long the legislative session lasted. The Assembly probably sat in two houses, and the Lower House consisted of ten members, of whom one, the Speaker, Captain Richard Ewens, was also a Commissioner.[5] Of the other nine, Captain Robert Vaughan came from Kent, Peter Sharp from Patuxent, Captain Robert Sly from St. Mary's.[6] Captain Joseph Weeks, Mr. Robert Taylor, Captain Thomas Besson, Captain Philip Morgan, Mr. Michael Brooke, and Mr. James Johnson are unidentified as to residence.

Bacon numbers thirteen chapters as the laws of this Assembly.[7] The first of these is a confirmation of the act of recognition of 1654, and the second is a repeal of four of the acts of that year, one of which, concerning sheriffs' and

---
[1] Bozman, II, 547; 3 Md. Arch., Coun., 331.
[2] 3 Md. Arch., Coun., 331.
[3] 1 Md. Arch., Ass., 359; Bozman, II, 549. On Samuel Preston, son of the first settler, see Penn and Logan Correspondence, II, 341.
[4] 10 Md. Arch., Prov. Ct., September (22) 519, (23) 521, (24) 524, (25) 527, (26) 534, (28) 542, (29) 542, (30) 544, October (1) 545, (5) 547.
[5] Andrew Skinner was clerk. Sly and Brooke had sat as Commissioners.
[6] See p. 107.
[7] 1 Md. Arch., Ass., 359-365, 1654, ch. 8, levies on visible estate; ch. 13, theft; ch. 16, births, marriages, and deaths; ch. 34, fees.

Josias Fendall, Governor, 1656. 111

Clerks' fees, is reenacted. "The public charges of this Province" for the year are to be levied by a poll tax, in which tax men-servants are included.[1] The tax was fixed at thirty-two pounds of tobacco per poll, which was slightly higher than the one of twenty-six pounds per poll laid in Virginia in 1654. A penalty was decreed for packing ground leaves or second crops of tobacco in any hogshead. Popleys or Poplar Island was annexed to Kent County. The inhabitants were allowed to use any lawful means for killing wolves, even employing an Indian for that purpose. The commission of the St. Mary's County court had not been attended to, and the Assembly levied on that county sums for the killing of thirteen wolves, for the sheriff's and Clerk's charges, for Mrs. Fenwick's "trouble and charge in entertaining and setting people over the river," etc. The charges, occasioned by "the disquiet and disturbance of the public peace of the Province" through Captain Josias Fendall's acts, whatever they may have been, were levied on the Province, as were those for the execution of servants at Providence who had killed Robert Parr,[2] their master. Other charges refer to the battle of the Severn: thus, Mr. Spry was paid for "diet and curing of wounded men;" Mr. Hodgkeys for "shoes and stockings delivered the soldiers in the service of Maryland;" the widow Besley for her relief, her husband being slain in the public service, leaving behind him four small children; John Wallcot "for attending and dressing 32 prisoners;" and Robert Franklin, John Underhill and George Whittle, who were wounded. Attachments and executions were so regulated as to be less oppressive to debtors. Captains Ewen, Besson, and Weeks were appointed as a committee to call to account any person who received or disposed of the fines "amerced upon any of the disturbers of the public peace in the last engagement." This seems to show that the order made in 1655 for the sequestra-

---
[1] Bozman (II, 550) thinks that negroes were not included but only indentured servants. Two servants, Stockden and Guneon, were freed from the poll tax.
[2] 10 Md. Arch., Prov. Ct., 554.

tion of the estates of members of the Proprietary party had not been honestly executed,[1] and this committee was directed to sit after the end of the Assembly's session, and also to receive from the sheriffs a just account of the fines, ransoms, or compositions received by them. The report of the committee must be made to Mr. Michael Brooke or Mr. Peter Sharp before the Provincial Court at Patuxent in March next, but we do not find it extant.

XII. Restoration of Proprietary Government, 1657.

Not until November 30, 1657, had articles of agreement been signed in England between Baltimore and Matthews, who represented "Bennett and other people in Maryland, now or late in opposition to his Lordship's government."[2] Ten days before this, Baltimore had sent new instructions to his Governor and Council.[3] The first of these authorized Fendall to accept the resignation of any Councilor who desired to tender it, and empowered any three of the Council, including Calvert, to discharge any Councilor who should refuse to act or to attend courts without excuse. A new great seal was sent out in Fendall's care, and he was given authority to affix it to patents, in accordance with the Conditions of Plantation, to which patents "Fendall and Calvert, or, if the latter die, 2 others of the Council," must sign their names. Persons receiving patents must take the oath of fidelity, as altered in accordance with the report of the Committee of Trade made September 16, 1656, and those who had opposed the Proprietary government must subscribe a submission thereto, in presence of the Governor or Secretary. A confirmation of a grant of ten thousand acres to Edward Eltonhead[4] was made. Fendall, Calvert, and any other two Councilors were empowered to make any foreigner capable of taking advantage of the Conditions of Plantation. Robert Clarke was reappointed

---

[1] Bozman, II, 550.
[2] 3 Md. Arch., Coun., 332.
[3] 3 Md. Arch., Coun., 335.
[4] Bozman (II, 556) queries whether he was Wm. Eltonhead's son.

Restoration of Proprietary Government, 1657.

as Councilor, and Fendall and Calvert were granted permission to add other Councilors, not exceeding six in number. In case of Philip Calvert's death, that early pioneer, Thomas Cornwallis,[1] was to take his place in confirming Fendall's acts. These instructions were doubtless drafted in anticipation of the agreement, which recited that the controversies in Maryland had led to "much bloodshed and great distempers there, endangering the utter ruin of that plantation." The matter had been referred to the English authorities, but Cromwell and the Privy Council had not as yet, "by reason of their great affairs," had leisure to determine the question, so that the inhabitants of Maryland "remain in a very sad, distracted and unsettled condition." In this juncture of affairs Edward Digges, who had been sent by Virginia as an additional agent a short time before, used his "friendly endeavors" about "the composure of the said differences,"[2] and so Baltimore agreed to treat, stipulating that the Puritan party should not execute any governmental act, should deliver up to the Governor or Secretary all the records of the Province, and the great seal, if they found it, and should submit to the Proprietary government for the future. If the Puritans agreed to this, on his part Baltimore would agree that the differences which had arisen in Maryland should not be decided in the Provincial Courts, but in such manner as Cromwell and his Council should direct; that the Puritans might have land patents just as if no controversy had occurred, provided they sued out the patents within nine months, took the oath of fidelity, and paid the usual fees; that such of the Puritans as wished to remove from Maryland might have a year to do so; and that the Proprietary would never consent to the repeal of the act of 1649 concerning religion. In other words, the Puritans yielded, and Samuel Matthews, that old enemy of the Pro-

---
[1] Bozman (II, 557) suggests that there is a slight distrust of Fendall here.
[2] Bozman, II, 552. The instructions of the Virginians to Digges direct him to assure Cromwell that they had not interested themselves in the quarrel in Maryland.

prietary, who had aided in the deposition of Governor Harvey because of his friendliness to Baltimore, had to sign this submission twenty years later. Bearing these papers with him,[1] Fendall returned to America, and on February 26 he resumed the titular Governorship. On the next day he held a Council at St. Mary's, at which Calvert and Stone were present and at which the articles between Baltimore and Matthews were published. Letters were then sent to Fuller, Preston, and the other Puritan leaders, asking them to meet Fendall, Calvert, and Cornwallis at "St. Leonard's Creek in Patuxent River," on March 18, to perform the articles. Bennett had received word of the agreement from Matthews and wrote of it at once to Fuller. Baltimore had, by lost instructions dated November 18, authorized Fendall and Calvert to treat with the Commissioners, and to ratify and confirm such articles as should be agreed upon with reference to the restoration of the Proprietary government.[2]

On March 18, 1657/8, the three Proprietary representatives came to St. Leonard's,[3] but wind and weather kept Captain Fuller back until Saturday the twentieth, when he came with Preston, Lloyd, Mears, Philip Thomas, and Samuel Withers to surrender the government. The day was far spent when they arrived, and, as Sunday was "not fit to treat of business," negotiations were begun on Monday, March 22. Fendall read the agreement and demanded that the records, great seal, and government of the Province be delivered to him, promising to carry out Baltimore's part of the agreement. He then read Baltimore's instructions of the preceding November.

Fuller and his Commissioners[4] propounded divers other articles tending, as they conceived, to the "quiet and welfare of the Province." These were debated during Monday

---
[1] 3 Md. Arch., Coun., 332.
[2] 3 Md. Arch., Coun., 334; 1 Md. Arch., Ass., 369.
[3] 3 Md. Arch., Coun., 335. On the early Proprietary land grants down to this period see Maryland Historical Magazine, III, 160.
[4] 3 Md. Arch., Coun., 339; 1 Md. Arch., Ass., 369.

and Tuesday. On Wednesday the amended articles, which had been engrossed, were read, and being approved by both sides, were signed by Fendall, Calvert, and the Commissioners, with many other persons.

"Then was the Governor's commission publicly read and proclaimed and writs issued immediately for an Assembly to be held at St. Leonard's 27° Aprilis following." Thus, at the beginning of the year 1658, O. S., was Baltimore's rule reinstated throughout the Province, as it had been established at the same time of year twenty-three years before. The articles here drawn up were enacted into law at the April session of the General Assembly and form the first chapter in that session's laws.

The first article declared that all persons on both sides should be indemnified and "freed from any charge or questioning for any act" done from December, 1649, to the date of the treaty. Fendall and his associates objected to this statement, as the words seemed to "admit of a necessity of pardon and, consequently, an implication of guilt in his Lordship's officers," but finally yielded, as they considered that "some of his Lordship's officers needed an indemnity for breach of trust passed."

The second article affirmed the legality of sheriffs', clerks', and secretarys' fees since 1652 and of the levies made by the General Assemblies of 1654 and 1657. The Proprietary's representatives adroitly said of this article that these Assemblies represented the "major part of the people," though not summoned "by lawful warrant," and that the "Proprietary is not bound to any one way of calling Assemblies, or assenting to what by them is done," so they agreed to the article.

The other articles stated that no person should be disarmed and "left to the cruelty of the Indians" unless he be "proved to bear arms to an hostile intent," that the conduct of any person since 1652 should not deprive him of the suffrage, or of the right to sit in the Assemblies; that no order of Assembly or court in cases of private law since 1654 "shall be declared void by pretence of irregularity of the power of government;" that land warrants should be granted to all entitled to them by the Conditions of Plantation who should apply for them within six months; and that a submission to Baltimore be substituted for the oath of fidelity in the case of persons then resident within the Province. The Proprietary's representatives agreed to the last article, with the clear understanding that the oath of fidelity must be taken by all not then residing in Maryland.

The struggle was over and Baltimore had won. Not unfairly does Browne sum up his policy in his history of Maryland:[1] "Every engine had been brought to bear against him—fraud, misrepresentations, religious animosities and force, and each for a time had succeeded. He owed his triumph to neither violence, fraud, nor intrigue; but to the justice of his cause and his wisdom, constancy, and patience."

---

[1] See p. 88.

APPENDIX.

A Summary of the Proceedings of the Provincial Courts, 1649 to 1658, Chronologically Arranged.

Provincial Courts of 1649 and 1650.

The Provincial Court met in June, 1649, probably in October, in November, and in December, on January 25, 1649/50, at St. Mary's with only Stone and Hatton present; on February 20 at the Governor's house in St. Michael's Hundred, when Price came as a third member; and at St. Mary's on February 26, when Greene took the place of Price.[1] The proceedings were of small interest for the most part; cases came up involving the title to cattle,[2] and deeds of heifers were formally recorded,[3] as were many earmarks of individuals.[4] Powers of attorney were registered, especially to George Manners, who seems to have been one of the first legal practitioners in the Province;[5] a commission was issued to administer an oath;[6] we find mortgages of crops, cattle, and vessels,[7] and releases[8] and indentures for servants.[9] Many suits were brought for debts of tobacco, of blue linen and of other goods, for the unlawful detention

---

[1] 4 Md. Arch., Prov. Ct., 485, 495, 538, 544, 546 (Nov. 15, Greene presided, and Price, Pile, Vaughan, and Hatton were also present), 527.
[2] 4 Md. Arch., Prov. Ct., 485, 497. Case for illegal detention of a bull, 4 Md. Arch., Prov. Ct., 540, 10 Md. Arch., Prov. Ct., 3, 4.
[3] 10 Md. Arch., Prov. Ct., 9, 13, 32, 48; 4 Md. Arch., Prov. Ct., 500, 508, 516, 527.
[4] 4 Md. Arch., Prov. Ct., 487, 495, 498, 500, 506, 508, 514, 515, 518, 536, 543, 547; 10 Md. Arch., Prov. Ct., 9.
[5] 4 Md. Arch., Prov. Ct., 485, 513, 518, 533, 536; 10 Md. Arch., Prov. Ct., 7, 8, 9.
[6] 4 Md. Arch., Prov. Ct., 507, 510, 515.
[7] Bonds were filed, 10 Md. Arch., Prov. Ct., 8; 4 Md. Arch., Prov. Ct., 512, 516.
[8] 4 Md. Arch., Prov. Ct., 518.
[9] 4 Md. Arch., Prov. Ct., 519.

of a crop, of a boat,[1] of a servant,[2] for slander,[3] concerning a warranty of a servant.[4] The custom of the country concerning servants who had served out their period of indenture was discussed,[5] writs were issued concerning persons intending to leave the Province and those who carried away fugitive debtors.[6] Probate matters also were attended to by the court.[7] A suit brought for assault and battery was submitted to arbitrators and their decision is recorded.[8] Among the more interesting items was a mortgage made by Sheriff Philip Land of St. Mary's County of the "whole benefit profit, and allowance" which shall come to him from his office "for this present year, together with a cow of his," as security for a debt.[9] In November, Greene lodged a complaint against "Skipper Abraham Janson" because he had, while "riding at an anchor in St. George's River" in the preceding March, "aboard his ship, publicly," abused Greene, who was then the Governor, "with most disgraceful and reproachful language," thereby not only endeavoring to impair Greene's reputation, but also to "affront his Lordship's dignity here."[10] Vaughan, with John Hatch, as Janson's attorney in the Province, thereupon requested Greene[11] to withdraw his charges, and Hatch promised to pay the costs incurred. Upon this Greene pardoned Janson and withdrew his action, "in a confident expectation" of Janson's better behavior

---

[1] 4 Md. Arch., Prov. Ct., 497.
[2] 4 Md. Arch., Prov. Ct., 496, 500.
[3] 4 Md. Arch., Prov. Ct., 498.
[4] 4 Md. Arch., Prov. Ct., 533, 537, 538.
[5] 4 Md. Arch., Prov. Ct., 539, see 10 Md. Arch., Prov. Ct., 48, 238.
[6] 4 Md. Arch., Prov. Ct., 533, 537, 540.
[7] 4 Md. Arch., Prov. Ct., Francis Cox's estate, 502; Wm. Wheatley's estate, 507; J. Thomson's estate, 499, 503; Thomas Hebden's will, 511, 519, 520, 548, 10 Md. Arch., Prov. Ct., 46, 418; Wm. Thompson's estate, 4 Md. Arch., Prov. Ct., 525, 534; P. Makarell's estate, 529; Thomas Arnold's will, 543.
[8] 4 Md. Arch., Prov. Ct., 485, 501, 505, 523, 538.
[9] 4 Md. Arch., Prov. Ct., 493, 502, 542; 10 Md. Arch., Prov. Ct., 5.
[10] 4 Md. Arch., Prov. Ct., 515, 517.
[11] They call him "now present Governor."

when he should come to Maryland again. A little afterwards, when Mrs. Brent sued Manners for a debt, he attempted to plead as set-off a fee for a service he as sheriff rendered to her as the Proprietary's attorney, but the set-off was not allowed, as the sheriff must execute all business belonging to his office which concerns Baltimore without fee.[1] Court procedure was becoming fixed and formal; defaults[2] and nonsuits appeared, and Bretton was blamed for tearing the draft of a deposition taken in a case.

In February, 1649/50, Sterman, who had been concerned in the plundering time on Ingle's side, complained of Richard Husbands, mariner, because he refused to give Sterman a bond he had promised.[3] John Dandy testified that he heard the promise and was also present at the refusal, at which time Husbands said: "You are lawless ashore and I will use what law I please here aboard. You long to raise a second Ingle here." Elias Beach sued Henry Adams for trespass in taking away his boat from his landing-place without license.[4] Adams admitted taking the boat, but said that there was no damage done, as he "did but directly cross the Creek therewith and immediately returned it again." Furthermore, he thought Beach had given him leave, for when he asked Beach for a passage, the answer was, "I would willingly give you passage, but think my boat is leaky and will not swim." Beach's attorney admitted that his client had not proceeded in this cause but for the counsel of "some ill neighbors," and that he could not prove any damage; but he asked that the case be respited till the next court, that the cause might be tried by another judge. After long debate Greene, "the present Governor," declared in favor of dismissing the case, as there was no proof of damages, and said that the plaintiff should have no more time, as the parties he wished as witnesses lived within a mile of him and two miles of the court, but had not been

---

[1] 4 Md. Arch., Prov. Ct., 529.
[2] 4 Md. Arch., Prov. Ct., 532, 539.
[3] 4 Md. Arch., Prov. Ct., 546.
[4] 4 Md. Arch., Prov. Ct., 487, 530, 547.

summoned. The postponement until Stone's return would "not only be a wilful delay of justice, but also secretly to admit a corruption in the present judge, much to the indignity of his Lordship's both Court and person." The other four Councilors present, however, voted to postpone the cause, that the plaintiff might prove his damage; they held that there must have been some damage, "were it but the wearing of the boat," and that it would be a dangerous precedent to decide such actions in behalf of the trespasser. They furthermore saw no danger of delay of justice, and Greene had to yield. When the case came up in February, Stone voted with Greene to dismiss it, as no damage was proved; but Hatton, the only other Councilor present, dissented.

An execution was granted in March to John Dandy for work done as a smith, in accordance with the law passed for the benefit of that artificer.[1] Only one case of fraud in the tobacco trade is reported. In February, 1649/50, oath was taken that little more than one hogshead of good tobacco had been found in two hogsheads which John Jarboe, a planter, packed.[2]

Provincial Courts, April and June, 1650.

During the spring and summer two courts were held:[3] the one in April and the other on June 25, the latter of which was held for only one day and then broken up until October, "upon the earnest motion of the inhabitants to be discharged of their attendance on the Court at present, it being very like to be plantable weather."[4] General powers of attorney were filed to Manners, who represented Mrs. Margaret Brent and others, one of these powers being merely for suits in which the principal was plaintiff.[5] Record was

---

[1] 10 Md. Arch., Prov. Ct., 7.
[2] 10 Md. Arch., Prov. Ct., 9.
[3] 10 Md. Arch., Prov. Ct., 15, 23, 27. Nicholas Gwyther was appointed sheriff on March 25, 10 Md. Arch., Prov. Ct., 10.
[4] On the court records we find earmarks recorded, 10 Md. Arch., Prov. Ct., 10, 13, 14, 18, 20, 23, 30, 42. An affidavit is recorded concerning the alteration of one of them, 10 Md. Arch., Prov. Ct., 29.
[5] 10 Md. Arch., Prov. Ct., 17, 19, 23, 24, 26.

Appendix. 121

made of nuncupative wills of Robert Wiseman and Henry Hooper, surgeon, and of other probate matters,[1] from which we learn that the allowance of a year and a day to an administrator was already a Provincial custom.[2] We also find a jointure of a dwelling-house, plantation, and four cows made by James Johnson to his wife Barbara, a kinswoman of Mr. Secretary Hatton.[3] Mortgages of crops,[4] assignments,[5] among them two of debts from tavern keepers for entertainment of Assemblymen,[6] and deeds of cows[7] are found, of course. Few crimes are noted; an appeal from the Kent County court judgment was allowed because the defendant was guilty of perjury;[8] John Dandy, the smith, sued Richard Husbands, mariner,[9] because on his ship in February he bound Dandy's arms behind him and tied them to his neck with a cord, in rigorous fashion; Thomas Maidwell sued Dandy and wife for assaulting him in a violent manner and striking him to the ground with a hammer,[10] because he had " accepted of 2 or 3 peaches"[11] from a girl who lived in Dandy's household; and a man was charged with stealing a parcel of peas, a cake of soap, a parcel of shot, and a bottle of vinegar, which he hid in a loft and in the corn.[12] A question of account was referred to arbitrators, that the differences might be determined or the arbitrators' proceedings certified for the court's further order.[13]

---

[1] 10 Md. Arch., Prov. Ct., 10, 11, 35 (21, administration of John Palmer's estate. He was of Kent), 30, Jas. Warrington's estate. Robt. Wiseman's estate, St. Mary's, April 16, 1650, Cotton, The Maryland Calendar of Wills.
[2] 10 Md. Arch., Prov. Ct., 23. Estate of Wm. Tompson.
[3] 10 Md. Arch., Prov. Ct., 12.
[4] 10 Md. Arch., Prov. Ct., 14, 19, 22.
[5] 10 Md. Arch., Prov. Ct., 18.
[6] 10 Md. Arch., Prov. Ct., 14.
[7] Among them one by Greene to his sons Francis and Thomas, 10 Md. Arch., Prov. Ct., 14, 20, 27, 29, 30.
[8] 10 Md. Arch., Prov. Ct., 17.
[9] 10 Md. Arch., Prov. Ct., 25.
[10] 10 Md. Arch., Prov. Ct., 31.
[11] This is the earliest reference to Maryland's peach industry. The suit was speedily compromised.
[12] 10 Md. Arch., Prov. Ct., 17.
[13] 10 Md. Arch., Prov. Ct., 25, 46, 47.

122   *Maryland Under the Commonwealth.*

A foreman of a jury was sued[1] because the loser by the decision claimed that the verdict was imperfect. While the cause was being heard, the plaintiff, William Hardwick, said that when the cause formerly came to hearing, Greene, who was Governor at the time, put him in prison to take him off from the prosecution. For these opprobrious words, as Greene was then sitting on the bench, the court fined Hardwick and committed him to imprisonment during the Governor's pleasure. Hardwick then expressed himself as very sorry and asked Greene's forgiveness in open court, and all penalties were remitted.

Two men claimed a gun which seems to have been taken from the plaintiff by Leonard Calvert, when he last went to Kent, upon promise to return it when he came back.[2] This promise was forgotten, and Calvert later gave the defendant the gun. The court awarded the plaintiff the gun, but divided the costs, as the defendant "had good reason to stand out to a trial." Mrs. Brent was directed to give over some cows which Calvert had given in payment for a house and plantation, and was secured in "quiet possession" of the land in return.[3] Mrs. Brent, as her brother's representative, was also sued for the hire of a shallop used in Calvert's last Kentish expedition.

Runaway servants[4] from Virginia were ordered to be returned to their masters, in care of the Virginia officer sent to secure them, and a curious case appeared in which a man complained against another for "detaining from him a boy heretofore taken by the Indians in the last massacre in Virginia and by them, since those wars, returned back to be presented to Sir William Berkeley, Governor there, who was pleased to give the boy" to the plaintiff. The defendant alleged that the boy was his own son, but failed to prove it,

---

[1] 10 Md. Arch., Prov. Ct., 26. Probably because the verdict was alleged not to be unanimous. The case was not settled.
[2] 10 Md. Arch., Prov. Ct., 24, 40. Other echoes of the difficulties of Calvert's times may be found on pp. 10-12.
[3] 10 Md. Arch., Prov. Ct., 15, 27. Calvert gave these cows by writing dated February 10, 1646/7.
[4] 10 Md. Arch., Prov. Ct., 15, 20, 24, 27, 35, 42.

Appendix. 123

and immediately after the trial the plaintiff filed an assignment of his right in the boy to the defendant.

PROVINCIAL COURT, SEPTEMBER, 1650, TO MARCH, 1651.

The Provincial Court met monthly from September, 1650, to March, 1651.[1] At the February court seven Councilors were present, the largest number yet recorded, but usually only three or four sat on the bench. Probate matters have some interesting features;[2] one administrator files an inventory and receives his quietus, a caveat is issued against a will, a widow is allowed maintenance from an estate for a year, administration of an estate is assigned. Some unfinished business concerning Leonard Calvert's estate is transacted. Thomas Hebden's widow fails in an attempt to oust the trustees of certain property appointed by her husband during his life, and on their complaint is forbidden to make any wilful waste of the estate.[3] The usual paucity of criminal matters is found, a case of assault and battery being the only one referred to.[4] A jury of inquest upon the body of a servant, who seems to have died in a fit, holds that his master is not responsible, but orders him to pay the costs of the jury, as he buried the servant privately and suddenly, and thus aroused suspicions.[5] In September, Brent is accused of acting prejudicially to the Proprietary's rights and Manners is ordered to investigate the charges, but nothing came of them.[6]

Cattle are sold,[7] one of them paying for certain books

---

[1] 10 Md. Arch., Prov. Ct., 33, 45, 51, 52, 54, 75, 157.
[2] 10 Md. Arch., Prov. Ct., 67. P. Mackerall's estate, 35, 42, 43. Wm. Porter's estate (Kent), 10 Md. Arch., Prov. Ct., 50, 62, 75, Cotton, Maryland Calendar of Wills. Nicholas Harvey's, 10 Md. Arch., Prov. Ct., 63. Nathaniel Stiles's estate, Cotton, Maryland Calendar of Wills. Other estates referred to are Robert Short (Kent), 10 Md. Arch., Prov. Ct., 62, Hy Crawley (whose will was dated 1639), 60, Edward Cummins (Kent), 43, 62. A guardian of Robert Short's daughter is appointed, 51.
[3] 10 Md. Arch., Prov. Ct., 37, 46, see 4 Md. Arch., Prov. Ct., 418, 512, 548.
[4] 10 Md. Arch., Prov. Ct., 51.
[5] 10 Md. Arch., Prov. Ct., 52, 73.
[6] 10 Md. Arch., Prov. Ct., 33.
[7] 10 Md. Arch., Prov. Ct., 34, 45, 52, 53, 55.

brought to the Jesuits,[1] earmarks are recorded,[2] and traffic seems to be covering other fields than cows and tobacco. Many debts are adjudicated, accounts adjusted,[3] judgments acknowledged,[4] acknowledgments and receipts entered on the records,[5] sureties accepted.[6] A bond is recorded,[7] set-offs are claimed.[8] A commission is issued to take testimony,[9] a case formerly decided is not allowed to be reopened,[10] many powers of attorney are filed and revoked,[11] cases are respited for such reasons as that witnesses are in Virginia[12] or the defendant is unable to travel.[13] A chattel mortgage,[14] a crop mortgage,[15] a deed of sale of a shallop,[16] a partnership bond for the hiring out of half a shallop,[17] are found. A man claims two hogsheads of tobacco, and states that one of those which the defendant gave him has been claimed by a third person.[18] The court orders half of the debt discharged, as the plaintiff had received one hogshead, and still another person agrees to pay the other for the defendant. A servant sues for his outfit according to the custom of the country.[19]

Cases of assumpsit appear[20] for work as a bricklayer[21] or a carpenter.[22] A man secures judgment against Robert

---

[1] 10 Md. Arch., Prov. Ct., 33.
[2] 10 Md. Arch., Prov. Ct., 45, 50, 64.
[3] 10 Md. Arch., Prov. Ct., 35–38, 40, 41, 66, 69, 71.
[4] 10 Md. Arch., Prov. Ct., 37, 38, 43, 50, 54.
[5] 10 Md. Arch., Prov. Ct., 53, 54, 63.
[6] 10 Md. Arch., Prov. Ct., 53.
[7] 10 Md. Arch., Prov. Ct., 64.
[8] 10 Md. Arch., Prov. Ct., 71.
[9] 10 Md. Arch., Prov. Ct., 64.
[10] 10 Md. Arch., Prov. Ct., 41.
[11] 10 Md. Arch., Prov. Ct., 39, 41, 43, 51, 59, 60, 63, 64.
[12] 10 Md. Arch., Prov. Ct., 36, 38, 39, 40, 47.
[13] 10 Md. Arch., Prov. Ct., 72.
[14] 10 Md. Arch., Prov. Ct., 59.
[15] 10 Md. Arch., Prov. Ct., 32.
[16] 10 Md. Arch., Prov. Ct., 51.
[17] 10 Md. Arch., Prov. Ct., 64.
[18] 10 Md. Arch., Prov. Ct., 39, 53, 66. See 65 for a curious case where two men disagreed about the proper delivery of tobacco to be paid for a rug.
[19] 10 Md. Arch., Prov. Ct., 48, 52. See 4 Md. Arch., Prov. Ct., 539.
[20] 10 Md. Arch., Prov. Ct., 35.
[21] 10 Md. Arch., Prov. Ct., 39, 46.
[22] 10 Md. Arch., Prov. Ct., 58. See 72, 73, for a suit for failure to perform contract to build a house.

Brooke, the Councilor, for tobacco due on specialty and for two bushels of onions.[1] The defendant had offered to make over a man-servant bound for four years and pay any remainder in tobacco, but the offer had been refused. Brooke seems to have been considerably indebted at this time, and several judgments were recovered against him.[2] Brooke was absent from the January and February courts, and at the latter, one of his creditors, who wished soon to return to Europe and to carry with him tobacco which Brooke owed him, induced the Council to summon Brooke and to promise relief if Brooke did not come. Brooke sent his son, Charles, as his attorney. The case proved to be a claim for the payment of the hire of two men-servants for thirteen weeks' labor.[3] Brooke denied that he owed aught, for the men were hired jointly for the time, and as one was absent from illness for five weeks of the thirteen, the covenant was not fulfilled by the plaintiff. A jury was impannelled and gave the plaintiff a judgment for the time the men had worked. A suit is found between two tenants on Gerard's manor concerning a lease of certain land there,[4] and Governor Stone sues Mrs. Brent for a sufficient conveyance of his house at St. Mary's.

A case of slander was filed in October[5] by Captain John Price, a Councilor, against Luke Gardiner for saying that he "kept an unlawful dog to kill his neighbors' stocks, because he would have the whole range himself." Gardiner declared that he added, "for aught I know," to the sentence, and that the words were not published, but spoken privately to Captain Price. The court, however, looked upon the words as a "disrespective expression to one of his Lordship's

---

[1] 10 Md. Arch., Prov. Ct., 58.
[2] 10 Md. Arch., Prov. Ct., 59. As no sheriff had been appointed for Brooke's county—Charles—until March 2, 1653, on that day Nicholas Gwyther, the sheriff of St. Mary's, was directed to collect the debt and do all sheriff's business for Charles County till further order, 10 Md. Arch., Prov. Ct., 124.
[3] 10 Md. Arch., Prov. Ct., 54–58. The servants belonged to Mitchell and had been working for Stone. Brooke sent them out to hunt, and they were lost in the woods.
[4] 10 Md. Arch., Prov. Ct., 36.
[5] 10 Md. Arch., Prov. Ct., 35, 38.

Council," though it "remitted the offence" on Gardiner's "acknowledgment of his fault." In another case Mrs. Francis Pope complained that Richard Browne had said that he learned from his wife that Mrs. Pope said that "the King died justly." This was a high matter, and the defendant was clearly "found in two several tales," and was fined for these and "for intermeddling in a business of this nature." Having won her cause, Mrs. Pope was merciful and remitted the fine, as Browne was a poor man, so he merely paid costs.

In March, 1650/1, George Manners was fined[1] for executing an attachment some time previously, alleging that Philip Land, the sheriff, had appointed him as his deputy, when in reality Land had appointed Nicholas Gwyther. At the same time Gwyther is reappointed sheriff until 1652, after which time the office is promised again to Land.

In November, William Eltonhead sued George Manners for slander,[2] but the latter brought witnesses to testify that Eltonhead had said that Governor Stone and Mr. Mottram had been better for the plundering (i. e., Ingle's attack), and that if they had been in England they would both have been hanged for selling powder and shot to the plunderers. Eltonhead alleged that there was a conspiracy against him, but Manners's death put an end to the case.

PROVINCIAL COURT, MAY, 1651, TO MARCH, 1651/2.

In the year following the session of the General Assembly we have record of the meeting of the court in the months of May, June, November, and December, 1651, and January, February, and March, 1651/2. Stone and Hatton were always present and sometimes sat alone, while at other times they were assisted by from two to five Councilors.[3]

A considerable amount of testamentary business is transacted. Thomas Greene died before January 20, 1651/2. On November 18, 1650, he assigned all his property to two

---
[1] 10 Md. Arch., Prov. Ct., 75.
[2] 10 Md. Arch., Prov. Ct., 156.
[3] May, 10 Md. Arch., Prov. Ct., 76; June, 76; Nov., 108; Dec., 113; Jan., 94, 123; Feb., 99; Mch., 140.

trustees for the benefit of his wife and children. At his death the Jesuits[1] should receive one thousand pounds of tobacco. If at the end of seventeen years his wife and children were dead, the trustees should take one fourth and the Jesuits the other three fourths of the estate, to be employed to charitable uses "most tending to the honor and glory of Almighty God, either here in this Province or elsewhere, my own decent livelihood during my life being herein always comprehended." George Manners, merchant and attorney at law, also died about this time, and his estate gave rise to much judicial business.[2] Mrs. Manners was administratrix and received wearing apparel, bed, bedding, and three barrels of corn "according to the custom of the Province," without inventory. Captain Edward Hill recovered from the estate three guns, which Copley had delivered to Manners to keep for Hill's use. Mrs. Manners married Edward Hall, her bondsman, an illiterate man. The notorious Captain Mitchell, who was a creditor of the estate, endeavored in November, 1652, to have Hall "discharged from any further meddling" with the administration, but

[1] "My most honored friend Thomas Copley, Esq., or his successors." 10 Md. Arch., Prov. Ct., 88, 123, 148, 160. Walter Cooper's estate, 10 Md. Arch., Prov. Ct., 83. Thos. Maidwell's estate, 10 Md. Arch., Prov. Ct., 122, 135, 144, 148, 162 (one of the claims against it was for payment for his transportation from England to Maryland); 163, his account with a curious medical bill is given.
[2] 10 Md. Arch., Prov. Ct., 93, 109, 113, 114, 119, 122, 127-130, 137, 144, 209, 216, 440, 453, 454, 460, 464, 467, 505. Cotton, Maryland Calendar of Wills. Nuncupative will of Mrs. Mary Risbrook of Kent, 10 Md. Arch., Prov. Ct., 91. Thos. Maidwell's estate, Cotton, Maryland Calendar of Wills. Thos. Weston's estate, 10 Md. Arch., Prov. Ct., 113. Mrs. Ann Cooper's estate, Cotton, Maryland Calendar of Wills. Wm. Brough's estate, Cotton, Maryland Calendar of Wills. Mrs. Katherine Hunt's estate, 10 Md. Arch., Prov. Ct., 113, Cotton, Maryland Calendar of Wills. Stephen Salmon, 10 Md. Arch., Prov. Ct., 113 (debt acknowledged to estate, execution to wait twelve months). John Garie's estate, 10 Md. Arch., Prov. Ct., 139. James Johnson's estate, Cotton, Maryland Calendar of Wills. Joseph Caille's estate, 10 Md. Arch., Prov. Ct., 139, 140, 144, 147, 169 (suit for salt), Cotton, Maryland Calendar of Wills. For quietus on Wm. Smithfield's estate see 10 Md. Arch., Prov. Ct., 17, 91, 4 Md. Arch., Prov. Ct., 466. Thomas Tynney of Providence is the first one of that part of the Province to have his estate administered. Leonard Strong was appointed administrator, 10 Md. Arch., Prov. Ct., 138, 156.

this seems not to have been done. In March, 1655/6, another creditor, who alleged that there was none to defend the estate, was appointed administrator de bonis non, but in May, 1657, Mrs. Thomas Orley, who had formerly been Mrs. Manners, but is now married for a third time, comes into court and has a discharge, as Hall had fully administered upon the estate ere he died, and had even paid out more than the estate amounted to.

There are three inquests, one in the case of Philip Anther, who was accidentally shot by James Longworth, for which the latter was fined five hundred pounds of tobacco;[1] a second over Thomas Lisle, who was killed by falling from a tree, in which he had climbed to cut a limb;[2] and a third over John Clifford, a servant, who was found drowned and was supposed to have committed suicide.[3]

Cattle continue a prominent feature in the people's life, and deeds of sale of cows,[4] or hogs,[5] of gift of cows,[6] and records of earmarks[7] appear, while controversies arise over the ownership of hogs,[8] over the killing of a hog[9] and of an offensive bull,[10] and over the sale of a cow represented falsely to be with calf.[11] Cattle are mortgaged[12] and sued for,[13] an estray is taken up;[14] but we see signs that land is becoming valuable, as well as the stock upon it. In addition to the familiar crop mortgages[15] we find a caveat filed for land,[16] and a controversy between Gerard and Lewis over rent of a plantation, which dispute they first brought before

---

[1] 10 Md. Arch., Prov. Ct., 139, 141.
[2] 10 Md. Arch., Prov. Ct., 154.
[3] 10 Md. Arch., Prov. Ct., 157.
[4] 10 Md. Arch., Prov. Ct., 84, 85.
[5] 10 Md. Arch., Prov. Ct., 86.
[6] 10 Md. Arch., Prov. Ct., 87, 108, 122.
[7] 10 Md. Arch., Prov. Ct., 83, 86, 87, 88, 93, 113, 122, 155, 156.
[8] 10 Md. Arch., Prov. Ct., 132.
[9] 10 Md. Arch., Prov. Ct., 100.
[10] 10 Md. Arch., Prov. Ct., 117.
[11] 10 Md. Arch., Prov. Ct., 119, 131.
[12] 10 Md. Arch., Prov. Ct., 153.
[13] 10 Md. Arch., Prov. Ct., 96, 146.
[14] 10 Md. Arch., Prov. Ct., 84.
[15] 10 Md. Arch., Prov. Ct., 82, 88, 91.
[16] 10 Md. Arch., Prov. Ct., 83.

Copley, from whose award Lewis appealed to a former judgment of the court.[1] He also stated that he had been "forced out of the Province by the late troubles," and asked that he be not obliged to pay rent for the time during which he could not use his plantation. The court allows the force of the defendant's pleas and gives a small judgment for Gerard. The manorial rents of three "tenements" have not been paid for three years, and the tenants are summoned to pay the arrears or suffer escheat of their lands.[2] A little later the Attorney General, Hatton, asks that the court see to the enforcement of the act of 1650 concerning deserted plantations and that the exception of orphans' lands from the act be not used to the Proprietary's injury.[3] The desired motion is made. Fixed fees are provided for the sheriff or his deputy, who go to levy for rents in arrears. A warrant is given the Surveyor to lay out one hundred acres for a man who transported himself to the Province in 1644,[4] two assignments of land are recorded,[5] and we find one deed of sale of all a man's property, "except my wearing clothes, and my wife's, my bed and all that belongs to it and 3 trunks with the goods contained in them, my whole crop of tobacco and my debts, one chamber pot and a pint pot and such of my books as I shall think fit."[6]

Debts[7] occupy much of the court's attention, assignments are made,[8] receipts recorded,[9] acknowledgments filed,[10] judgments confessed,[11] bonds filed,[12] and security is given.[13]

---

[1] 10 Md. Arch., Prov. Ct., 81.
[2] 10 Md. Arch., Prov. Ct., 93, 95.
[3] 10 Md. Arch., Prov. Ct., 125.
[4] 10 Md. Arch., Prov. Ct., 95, cf. 102.
[5] 10 Md. Arch., Prov. Ct., 101, 137.
[6] 10 Md. Arch., Prov. Ct., 119. Among things sold is a "yearling bull supposed to be in the woods."
[7] 10 Md. Arch., Prov. Ct., 79, 94–103, 108, 113, 123, 126, 166, 154, 129, 136, 146.
[8] 10 Md. Arch., Prov. Ct., 123.
[9] 10 Md. Arch., Prov. Ct., 93.
[10] 10 Md. Arch., Prov. Ct., 93, 94, 113.
[11] 10 Md. Arch., Prov. Ct., 76, 140.
[12] 10 Md. Arch., Prov. Ct., 83, 84, 112.
[13] 10 Md. Arch., Prov. Ct., 101, 102, 108, 128, 137, 144.

Thomas Chynne, a mariner and a mate on a ship which was ready to sail, sues for a debt of tobacco, which the debtor alleges he could not pay "till there be a season for striking tobacco," but in spite of this plea, judgment is given.[1] While the court acts with fair promptness,[2] cases are sometimes respited or postponed to a later court.[3] Many powers of attorney are filed,[4] an appeal is taken from a decision of the Anne Arundel County court,[5] a search warrant is issued,[6] and a man is given license to go to Virginia.[7] A gambling debt is not allowed to be recovered,[8] or one for hire for a voyage to Virginia or for other service to the use of "the Rebellion" of 1645. A man is whipped[9] for saying to one of the Governor's messengers: "You have an honest face. It is a pity you will be hanged," and "I wish the Virginians that came up in service of the Governor had estates in Virginia. Rather than I would have come up upon such employment as they did, I would have gathered oysters for my living." One case of a slander is tried,[10] the ownership of a small boat is determined,[11] and an unsuccessful suit is brought for hire of a boat.[12] Outside of Mitchell's case, there was little crime. A man was fined for striking another near the court door,[13] another had bound over to keep the peace a man whom he alleged to have threatened his life and to be living in adultery with his wife.[14]

One case of fraud comes up, in which it is alleged that

---

[1] 10 Md. Arch., Prov. Ct., 140. For an execution and set-off, see 10 Md. Arch., Prov. Ct., 135.
[2] In one case it refused to delay for a jury trial, but gave immediate judgment, 10 Md. Arch., Prov. Ct., 147.
[3] 10 Md. Arch., Prov. Ct., 80, 131, 203.
[4] 10 Md. Arch., Prov. Ct., 78, 121, 122, 137–139, 152.
[5] 10 Md. Arch., Prov. Ct., 103.
[6] 10 Md. Arch., Prov. Ct., 95.
[7] 10 Md. Arch., Prov. Ct., 98.
[8] 10 Md. Arch., Prov. Ct., 96, 97.
[9] 10 Md. Arch., Prov. Ct., 94.
[10] 10 Md. Arch., Prov. Ct., 115. Defendant said that plaintiff got one of his negroes with child.
[11] 10 Md. Arch., Prov. Ct., 103, 104, 115.
[12] 10 Md. Arch., Prov. Ct., 140.
[13] 10 Md. Arch., Prov. Ct., 136.
[14] 10 Md. Arch., Prov. Ct., 109.

a debt was paid in "deceitful rotten tobacco."[1] Copley is convicted, after a jury trial, of giving entertainment to and unlawfully detaining a runaway servant of a Virginia planter.[2] Questions with reference to contracts of service[3] and whether a man is a servant or not[4] are decided. Stone had possessed himself of Mrs. Margaret Brent's house at St. Mary's and she had offered to secure him against all just claims.[5] On July 22, 1650, she had written to recall to his mind her request that he find from the records what right she had to the house. She wished to advise with her brother before she gave Stone a deed, and stated that, if her title were not good, she would return the house into the inventory of Leonard Calvert, to whom it had belonged, and "would not entangle myself in Maryland, because of the Lord Baltimore's disaffections to me and the instructions he sends against us."[6] When she comes down, she promises to bring a copy of the statute to justify her right to Leonard Calvert's land, and hopes to have the matter tried in the Maryland court. Some trouble develops, and Giles Brent, as his sister's attorney, on January 5, 1651/2, gives Stone notice to leave the house.[7] Instead of doing so, however, he buys it from her on January 23, 1651/2.[8]

PROVINCIAL COURT, SPRING AND SUMMER OF 1652.

After the reduction of the Province by the Parliamentary Commissioners, a court for the County of St. Mary's was held on April 22, Mr. Robert Brooke and Lieutenant Richard Banks sitting as justices.[9] The court seems, however, to have performed all the functions of the Provincial one. It heard cases of alleged debt for tobacco or pork,[10] giving a

---

[1] 10 Md. Arch., Prov. Ct., 152.
[2] 10 Md. Arch., Prov. Ct., 132.
[3] 10 Md. Arch., Prov. Ct., 115, 117, 121, 127, 137.
[4] 10 Md. Arch., Prov. Ct., 144.
[5] 10 Md. Arch., Prov. Ct., 104.
[6] Stone is directed to sell the goods he has of hers.
[7] 10 Md. Arch., Prov. Ct., 122.
[8] 10 Md. Arch., Prov. Ct., 172.
[9] 10 Md. Arch., Prov. Ct., 159.
[10] 10 Md. Arch., Prov. Ct., 159, 160.

132   Maryland Under the Commonwealth.

jury trial in one case against Captain Mitchell, it relieved a man from a bond,[1] granted letters of administration and attended to other testamentary business,[2] recorded a release of an indentured servant,[3] and respited a suit[4] for a debt for money given a shipmaster to be laid out in Holland for commodities. Captain Mitchell's conduct came up for discussion, but his trial, of which we have already written, occurred at a second session of the county court held in June.[5] An assignment of debts and of a sloop to save a fellow bondsman from loss,[6] receipts,[7] debts of tobacco and cows,[8] trespass in driving away a bull,[9] a mortgage, and a gift of cows[10] are mingled with the serious business of the trial of the charges against Mitchell. A man is convicted of defaming another falsely by charging him with altering the earmarks of a parcel of pigs.[11] Francis Brooke alleged that John Dandy "unlawfully detained a parcel" of cows, which had originally been given him as security for a debt, now paid. Dandy said that he had paid the debt, and so claimed the cattle. The case dragged on for nearly a year, and then the court found that Brooke had paid nearly all the amount due, and decreed that he should have the cattle returned him when he paid the residue.[12]

On July 14, 1652, a court was held upon a special warrant,[13] and was attended by Stone, Hatton, Yardley, and

---

[1] 10 Md. Arch., Prov. Ct., 161.
[2] Estate of Wm. Brough, 10 Md. Arch., Prov. Ct., 162, 165, of Robert Ward, 10 Md. Arch., Prov. Ct., 161.
[3] 10 Md. Arch., Prov. Ct., 165.
[4] In June the jury gave plaintiff a verdict, 10 Md. Arch., Prov. Ct., 162, 166.
[5] On the last day of June, Stone, Hatton, Chandler, and Yardley held court instead of Brooke and Banks, but it is the "same court continued."
[6] 10 Md. Arch., Prov. Ct., 172.
[7] 10 Md. Arch., Prov. Ct., 170.
[8] 10 Md. Arch., Prov. Ct., 166-169.
[9] 10 Md. Arch., Prov. Ct., 167.
[10] 10 Md. Arch., Prov. Ct., 168.
[11] 10 Md. Arch., Prov. Ct., 167.
[12] 10 Md. Arch., Prov. Ct., 169, 195, 196, 209, 215, 224, 229, 256. The defendant had some cause to question the payment, so the costs were divided.
[13] 10 Md. Arch., Prov. Ct., 186. The cattle and land of the late

Chandler, to decide whether two indentured servants were entitled to freedom. They had belonged to Thomas Copley and his successors, that is, the Jesuits, and as Copley had recently died, Father Lawrence Starkey had the men arrested, as servants neglecting their employment. They set up a discharge, by agreement with Copley that they were to make a crop and pay certain quantities of tobacco to him, but, "by reason of much rain, the plants had been drowned." The court held that a bargain "betwixt the Master and his apprentice servants was of no validity at law," that the agreement was void, and that the men must serve out their "times of service."

PROVINCIAL COURTS, NOVEMBER, 1652, TO MARCH, 1653.

During the autumn of 1652 and the winter following, courts were held in November, January, and March.[1] The court records are quite full for this period and show an increasing variety of legal business. Earmarks were still entered,[2] deeds of sale or of gift of cattle were recorded,[3] and a cow was mortgaged with a plantation.[4] A suit was brought for delivery of the same useful animals[5] according to alleged agreement, and another case concerned the shooting of a bull.[6] Wild cattle caused great inconvenience, and Cornwallis, Eltonhead, Fenwick, and others asked the Provincial Court that these might be "killed or otherwise secured from annoyance," but Baltimore's attorney "claimed some right" in these cattle, and the matter was judged to

---

William Brough were sold, and the deed, with a power of attorney from the sellers, Wm. Scott, mariner, and wife (formerly Brough's wife), to the purchaser are recorded about this time, 10 Md. Arch., Prov. Ct., 187; see 169, 193, 195, 204, as to debts of the estate. Finally, the purchaser, Walter Beane, was ordered to take out letters of administration. Cotton, Maryland Calendar of Wills.

[1] November (20) 10 Md. Arch., Prov. Ct., 191; (23) 199; (24) 198, 203; (25) 207; January (20) 217; (21) 220; March (11) 232; (22), 237.
[2] 10 Md. Arch., Prov. Ct., 187, 189, 190, 197, 236, 249.
[3] 10 Md. Arch., Prov. Ct., 190, 213, 249.
[4] 10 Md. Arch., Prov. Ct., 198.
[5] 10 Md. Arch., Prov. Ct., 205.
[6] 10 Md. Arch., Prov. Ct., 246.

be of "such general concernment" as fitly to be referred to the General Assembly.[1] A year later, there having been no Assembly in the meantime, Governor Stone issued a proclamation reciting that Marks Pheypo, Nicholas Keating, Martin Kirke, and others had, "in a bold, contemptuous, unwarrantable manner gotten up, killed or disposed of to their own use" some of these wild cattle, and therefore, "in the name of the Keepers of the Liberties of England by authority of Parliament and as governor here under the Right Honorable Lord Baltimore, Lord Proprietary of this Province," Stone directed the above named men and all others to forbear from such conduct in future and to turn loose any such cattle now in their pens.[2] Gerard sued Fenwick for a colt and recovered one thousand pounds of tobacco when it was shown that the colt was dead.[3] Disputed titles to hogs,[4] and allegations that Robert Brooke had unlawfully slain another man's hogs, that other men had slain his,[5] and that men, by unlawfully hunting hogs on Kent Island, frightened and scattered Dr. Ward's pigs,[6] show how important were these animals.

Deeds of land are found, for example one of a parcel of two hundred acres, bearing the name of St. Jerome's Thicket, while several cases concerning title to land occur.[7] In one of these we find that the owner had "peach trees and other fruit trees" planted upon the cleared ground, an early instance of the raising of fruit, for which Maryland has always been famous.[8] In another case the defendant was accused of altering his bound marks, and Clarke, the Surveyor General, testified that this had been done by his direction, on account of a mistake in the survey.[9] The court

---

[1] 3 Md. Arch., Coun., 295.
[2] 10 Md. Arch., Prov. Ct., 324, lease referred to General Assembly.
[3] 10 Md. Arch., Prov. Ct., 238, 276, 354.
[4] 10 Md. Arch., Prov. Ct., 205, 225, 246.
[5] 10 Md. Arch., Prov. Ct., 220, 239, 240, 242, 243, 273, 353, 354.
[6] Without the precincts of the Lord Proprietor's forest, 10 Md. Arch., Prov. Ct., 233.
[7] 10 Md. Arch., Prov. Ct., 189, see 230.
[8] 10 Md. Arch., Prov. Ct., 198.
[9] 10 Md. Arch., Prov. Ct., 205, 218, 245. A verbal grant of land

Appendix. 135

directed the plaintiff peaceably to enjoy his land. If he prove, upon a new survey, to have more land than the former survey stated, he should have the additional land granted him on payment of the rent to the Proprietary. The Surveyor must pay the cost of this new survey, and each party must bear his own costs in the suit. In a third case Mrs. Edward Cummins, while a widow, had sold land to Joseph Weeks and afterwards married Dr. Thomas Ward. Weeks refused to perform his part of the bargain without a grant[1] of the land from the Proprietary, and the question arose as to whether the widow could sell the land " from her children, as it was part of her husband's estate granted by him to her and her heirs." As the estate was a freehold, the court held that the sale was lawful, and with Ward's consent directed that the proceeds of the sale should be "disposed of for the maintenance and best benefit" of Cummins's children. At the next court Ward complained of Weeks's "unconscionable and extreme dealing" in taking a servant in execution, leaving Ward with none, though Ward tendered other good satisfaction in cattle. The servant, he further alleged, belonged to the Cummins children. The case was referred to the Kent court to regulate the matter "in point of equity," as the county court "shall think fit."

Fugitives from debt[2] were a cause of trouble. Two men bought a sloop, giving a mortgage on their crops for payment, and went out of the Province on the vessel. Other

---

conflicted with a survey and was upheld, but the owner had to pay 300 pounds of tobacco and costs and survey charges and the rights of an equal amount of land to the complainant, 10 Md. Arch., Prov. Ct., 220.

[1] 10 Md. Arch., Prov. Ct., 228, 235. Robert Brooke also petitioned that a survey he alleged to be fraudulent be declared void, 10 Md. Arch., Prov. Ct., 245, 248. A warrant was granted Capt. Wm. Hawley for six thousand acres of land, to which Jerome Hawley had rights, but which had not been taken up by him, 10 Md. Arch., Prov. Ct., 250.

[2] One of the claims against the fugitives was assigned to the receiver of customs to pay dues to the Proprietary, 10 Md. Arch., Prov. Ct., 187, 188, 200, 201, 247. See case of Thomas Hamper, who left the Province, 10 Md. Arch., Prov. Ct., 201.

creditors appeared and their whole estate was attached. Cornwallis sued John Pile for transporting his cattle from Accomac[1] in 1643, and Pile showed a discharge from Fenwick, Cornwallis's agent, dated in 1647. This was given, as Fenwick testified, because Argall Yardley promised satisfaction in goods for the debt when his Dutch ship should come in, but the satisfaction was never given. The court held that the suit should be dismissed with costs and one hundred pounds of tobacco damages to Pile for his charges and trouble, but he remitted this sum in open court. The notorious Captain Mitchell sued one Major Levin Buskin for nails[2] and other materials furnished for the latter's house, and as Fenwick, Buskin's agent, admitted the debt,[3] Mitchell was given possession of the house and plantation until the debt should be paid. Governor Stone sued one William Empson for truck given him "to put amongst the Indians," and the Provincial Court referred the case to the arbitration of three men not members of the Council, who brought in a verdict for Stone, whereupon the court ordered

---

[1] 10 Md. Arch., Prov. Ct., 191, see 4 Md. Arch., Prov. Ct., 323. Cornwallis (10 Md. Arch., Prov. Ct., 190, 198, 207) sued Mrs. Hebden for a debt of her late husband's, secured by mortgage of cattle in 1643, and recovered a part of the amount hitherto unpaid.

[2] 10 Md. Arch., Prov. Ct., 193, 196, 210. Col. Yardley sued successfully Capt. Richard Husbands of the ship *Hopeful Adventure* for supplies of food furnished him, 10 Md. Arch., Prov. Ct., 197, 202, 390. Another skipper, Jacob Derickson, was sued for not bringing in goods, 10 Md. Arch., Prov. Ct., 247.

[3] There are several confessions of judgment recorded, 10 Md. Arch., Prov. Ct., 199, 206, 208, 209, 221, and also a suit to recover the balance of a bill where defendant had sent an insufficient amount of tobacco, 10 Md. Arch., Prov. Ct., 199. A man is sued as having undertaken to pay another's debt for him, 10 Md. Arch., Prov. Ct., 193, 201, 221. Other cases of debt are found: 10 Md. Arch., Prov. Ct. (1) 202, 249, 271, (2) 207, (3) 208, (4) 209, 217, a servant of Montjoy Evelin, in the possession of Gerard, was attached by the sheriff to pay Evelin's debt, and Gerard promised to secure him until the next court, (5) 221, 275, 338, a specialty sued on, (6) 222, 228, judgment assigned, (7) 222, Richard Bennett, Governor of Virginia, sues and recovers debt but no interest, (8) 238, defendant denies borrowing hogshead of tobacco, but says that he agreed to transport such hogshead for plaintiff to Virginia, but the tobacco proved rotten and unmerchantable, (9) 241, 277, 345, 366, covenant, (10) 249, receipt.

Empson to pay the amount[1] which the arbitrators found to be due.

One case, which was a claim for payment for some goods, was postponed[2] from November to January court upon the "defendant's wife's motion." Comparatively little testamentary business appeared.[3] Servants took up considerable time. Mary Jones complained of harsh usage from William Eltonhead and his wife and was ordered to return home with them. They were ordered, however, not to meddle with her "for matter of correction, but to sell or exchange her with all convenient speed."[4] A brickmaker sued Gerard for the house and equipment promised him at the expiration of his term of service, and in answer Gerard said that the plaintiff had run away and purloined some of his goods. The court, with the consent of the parties, annulled all contracts and suits between the parties and compelled the plaintiff to pay the costs.[5] In another suit[6] the plaintiff complained that the defendant did not deliver him as able a servant as he should have done in exchange for one of the plaintiff's. A jury brought in a verdict for the plaintiff, but the court ordered him to pay the "court charges," as he had kept the servant "so long without seeking for recompense and as the defendant had been at some charge in curing the servant . . . of a sore foot."

A servant of one of the Jesuits complained that his master "would keep him a perpetual servant," and he was

---

[1] 10 Md. Arch., Prov. Ct., 220.
[2] Mitchell finally acted as defendant's attorney, 10 Md. Arch., Prov. Ct., 203, 227.
[3] J. Cornish, Cotton, Maryland Calendar of Wills. Joseph Cadle's estate, land appraised and debt ordered paid, 10 Md. Arch., Prov. Ct., 190, 203, 208. Francis White's estate (Kent), 194, 230. John Gaither's estate (Anne Arundel), 194. Wm. Brough's estate, 169, 204. Robt. Ward's estate, 213. Wm. Stephenson's estate, 250, Cotton, Maryland Calendar of Wills. Anthony Rawlings, Cotton, Maryland Calendar of Wills.
[4] 10 Md. Arch., Prov. Ct., 191.
[5] 10 Md. Arch., Prov. Ct., 213, 237, 248, 271.
[6] 10 Md. Arch., Prov. Ct., 216, 223, 224. In another suit the plaintiff demands damages (10 Md. Arch., Prov. Ct., 237) because he had to pay a Virginian for bringing the defendant to Maryland, the defendant claiming to be a freeman.

directed to serve for three years, at the end of which time he should receive a cow, a sow, corn, and clothes, according to the custom of the country.[1] A man sued Fenwick for a servant promised him, and Fenwick pleaded that none had "come in"[2] from England. He did not satisfy the debt, and finally an execution against his body was issued, under which the Governor appointed the house of Henry Fox for a prison and ordered Fenwick not to depart out of the limits of this prison, which limits were half a mile from the house, till he paid the debt.

A curious deposition was filed concerning a hunting voyage.[3] One Ralph Harellton swore that in November, 1651, Paul Simpson, who was intending such an expedition, but could not speak the Indian language, came to Lieutenant William Lewis, Harellton's master, at Port Tobacco, his residence, and asked Lewis to join with him and share equally the meat they killed. Lewis agreed, and leaving his own boat, put guns and ammunition, two barrels of salt, and a "tun of cask" on Simpson's vessel. Simpson, Lewis, and Harellton went up the river on her toward Piscataway, and learning that there were some of the Apomattocks men hunting there, they took on board their goods, namely, three and one half tuns of cask, salt, guns, and meat. Lewis then asked Simpson to meet him at Guigawatick and to take on board the vessel at Piscataway the venison from ten deer which belonged to him. This was done, and Lewis provided a house and Indians for Simpson at Guigawatick and there settled him and Harellton. Simpson then told Lewis that he might return home and that, on Simpson's return from hunting, he would put in at Port Tobacco and divide with Lewis the meat which was killed, besides giving Copley a share out of Simpson's portion. Lewis next went down to St. Mary's to fetch up cattle, and Simpson asked him to

---

[1] 10 Md. Arch., Prov. Ct., 247. Another servant succeeded in a suit against Father Starkey for the equipment due him at the expiration of his term of service, 10 Md. Arch., Prov. Ct., 254, 277.
[2] 10 Md. Arch., Prov. Ct., 247, 365.
[3] 10 Md. Arch., Prov. Ct., 192.

bring some powder from Copley. Harellton had been left with Simpson, being charged to do whatever Simpson commanded him, and he was soon bidden also to go to St. Mary's and fetch powder from Copley. Simpson ordered Harellton that he must not speak to nor go to Lewis, and that he must not tell Copley that they had killed any fowl, though there was a hogshead of them when Harellton went down the river. At that time Simpson also had almost four hogsheads of venison, and one of Lewis's barrels of salt was untouched. Just at this time Simpson was in a good deal of trouble. He asked that Walter Pakes be bound over to keep the peace, and accused him of having stabbed him in the side and cut him in the arm.[1] This attack was made because Pakes charged Simpson with having committed adultery with his wife. But they soon made up, the bond was released, and on September 20, 1653, they signed articles of a general partnership with each other of the most extensive kind.

Comparatively few cases of tort are found. Three persons were accused of having said, about 1649, that they had "found a way to pay Eltonhead without weight or scales. Hang them, Papists dogs, they shall have no right here. It it not fit they should, for the Governor cannot abide them, but from the teeth outwards." To this truculent language[2] a bystander replied, "Fie, fie, you may be ashamed to judge so harshly upon Christians." Two men appealed from judgments of the Kent County court[3] in cases of slander. In one case the defendant was ordered to acknowledge in open court of the county that he had done the slandered woman great wrong and to ask her forgiveness, and to pay one thousand pounds of tobacco as fine, or, if his estate

---

[1] 10 Md. Arch., Prov. Ct., 188, 190, 203, 296, 320. On January 3, 1653/4, Pakes executed an instrument releasing Paul Simpson, Gent., "late of the Province of Maryland," from all claims which Pakes might have against Simpson and annulling any letters of attorney he had given him. See 321. Three powers of attorney are recorded in the latter part of 1652 and beginning of 1653, 10 Md. Arch., Prov. Ct., 221, 229, 246.
[2] 10 Md. Arch., Prov. Ct., 229, see 300.
[3] 10 Md. Arch., Prov. Ct., 234.

would not satisfy this, to be whipped with one and thirty stripes. The other appeal was referred to the General Assembly. The sheriff of Kent County was accused of malfeasance in office in not turning over to the Secretary fees due that officer, and was ordered to pay them at once.[1] Captain Vaughan, the commander of the county, had put the sheriff in office, and if the sheriff proved insolvent, Secretary Hatton was permitted to proceed against Vaughan.

In January the question[2] arose as to whether the rents payable to the Proprietary began "from the time of the survey or the delivery of the grant, and whether any rent ought to be paid for the year, wherein the land was surveyed, in case the survey was not made for 12 months or near thereabouts before the day of payment." The Council, after hearing evidence, unanimously decided that "rents were accountable from the date of the certificate of survey," and that, when the survey was made within twelve months before the rent day, the rent should be apportioned.

The court was careful of its dignity and fined men for being drunk or swearing in its august presence,[3] but mercifully postponed suits when one of the defendants was a woman lying in childbed[4] and when another one was a man disabled by some hurt. A number of bonds are recorded,[5] among them one for bail, another agreeing to submit a case to arbitration, and a third by which George Evelin created an annuity of £20 sterling in return for the cash sum of £120.

Stone and Hatton sued[6] one William Battan for selling liquor without a license, "contrary to the law of England," and for entertaining Stone's overseer to drink in his house, whereby he did neglect his business in sowing tobacco seed, by which omission the Governor was damnified. Battan was fined on the former charge, and then asked Hatton to mediate with the Governor on his behalf as to the latter one.

---

[1] 10 Md. Arch., Prov. Ct., 232.
[2] 10 Md. Arch., Prov. Ct., 223, see 203.
[3] 10 Md. Arch., Prov. Ct., 201, 221.
[4] 10 Md. Arch., Prov. Ct., 202, 229, 243.
[5] 10 Md. Arch., Prov. Ct., 211, 231, 237.
[6] 10 Md. Arch., Prov. Ct., 219, 243.

Appendix. 141

The court now clearly acts as an equity tribunal,[1] for example deciding a case concerning a lost bill. In one of the equity cases, that of Cornwallis v. Sterman, for carrying away goods in the plundering year, the defendants pleaded the statute of limitations, and as this was "doubtfully understood," the case was respited until the next General Assembly.[2] In March, 1653/4, however, the case was referred to the arbitration of Stone and Hatton, and was decided by directing the Stermans to pay three hogsheads and one hundred pounds of tobacco and court charges, whereupon Cornwallis should deliver them two bills given to Ingle concerning powder and a gun. An assignment from Ingle to Cornwallis of all his debts in Maryland had been made in England on September 8, 1647, "after a long and chargeable suit," and it was recorded in Maryland in January, 1652/3, with an inventory of sixteen debts, bearing various dates between 1640 and 1645.[3] Cornwallis at once brought suit on two of these claims against Gerard and Sterman. The case against Gerard was respited until April, if there should be no earlier General Assembly to consider it, that against Sterman[4] was postponed until the next court, "and the records to be searched in the meantime, to see whether any act of attainder were passed here against" Ingle. Gerard brought suit in turn against Fenwick,[5] as Ingle's former attorney, claiming that he had paid him. Ingle admitted payment, but demanded that he might see the bill on which Cornwallis had sued Gerard, that he might know whether it was the one upon which Cornwallis now sued. This was allowed, and Cornwallis was directed to bring the bill into court.

---

[1] 10 Md. Arch., Prov. Ct., 242, 246, 254. On the early development of equity see Newbold, Notes on the Introduction of Equity Jurisdiction into Maryland, 1634–1720.
[2] 10 Md. Arch., Prov. Ct., 219, 254 (in another case, in which Cornwallis was defendant, he pleaded limitations and won partly for this cause, 4 Md. Arch., Prov. Ct., 539; 10 Md. Arch., Prov. Ct., 238), 321, 348 (three hundred and fifty pounds in each hogshead).
[3] 10 Md. Arch., Prov. Ct., 211, 218, 238; 3 Md. Arch., Coun., 292.
[4] Cornwallis, 10 Md. Arch., Prov. Ct., 218, also sued Sterman for mismarking a cow.
[5] 10 Md. Arch., Prov. Ct., 241, 273, 275, 341.

In June the case of Cornwallis v. Gerard was referred to the General Assembly, but it came again before the Provincial Court and was decided on March 4, 1653/4. It was then determined that Gerard had gone to Virginia, after he knew of Ingle's conveyance to Cornwallis, and "unlawfully and, by the arbitrary power and favor of the then Governor there [probably Berkeley], obtained a judgment and thereby possessed himself of Ingle's estate in that Province." Here is a complicated affair which "tends to the questioning of the power of the late Governor of Virginia and to the reversing of a judgment already passed in that Colony concerning an estate then in that Colony, by opposing a conveyance made in England against that judgment." To prevent "clashing of contradictory orders" or engendering "any breach or just distaste betwixt the two governments, but rather, by all fair and friendly means, to preserve a mutual correspondency,". the court refused to proceed further, but referred Cornwallis to seek relief in Virginia, and if he did so and the Virginia court ordered Gerard to appear before it, his refusal to appear "will be understood as a contempt of the government here." If Cornwallis failed to prosecute the case in Virginia or lost it there, the Maryland court would see that he paid the costs.

At this time Baltimore made a claim[1] to part of Virginia, thinking that Acquia Creek was the South Branch of the Potomac, and at James City on March 14, 1653/4, Giles Brent presented a petition asking relief, inasmuch as Baltimore had instructed his Secretary to issue to another a grant of Brent's land in Westmoreland County. The Virginia Council ordered that the commissioners of that county guard the bounds and interests of Virginia, and we hear no more of the matter.

---

[1] William and Mary College Quarterly, XIII, 279, XVI, 34. On the Brents see also Virginia Magazine of History and Biography, XV, 450, article by W. B. Chilton.

Provincial Court, April to September, 1653.

In the sessions of court which were held in April, June, and September, 1653, varied business was transacted.[1] A case was postponed because the defendant suffered a "disastrous accident" by a boar,[2] earmarks were registered,[3] discharges of debts and acknowledgments were recorded.[4] One of the latter was to the smith, John Dandy, for fixing arms.[5] There was an inquest upon a suicide, whose estate is forfeited to the Proprietary,[6] and debts were proved against the estates of men who had died.[7] A bastardy case occupied much of the court's time in June,[8] and a special court, composed of Stone and Hatton, was held on August 8 to try a man committed by the Kent County court for felony, in that he broke open his master's chest and took goods out, intending to run away with them to Virginia.[9] He changed his mind and told his master that the Indians had opened the chest, and did not remove the goods from the house, so the court limited his punishment to twenty-five lashes and payment of court charges. The disreputable Captain Mitchell sued a former servant of his,[10] who had run away and, having been taken in execution by virtue of a judgment against Captain Mitchell, was appraised as having "two crops" to serve, whereas he really ought to have served for three years. Mitchell's contention was upheld, and the defendant was ordered to enter his service till he should give security to pay eight hundred pounds of

---

[1] April 10, 10 Md. Arch., Prov. Ct., 258. June 7, 8 and 9, 10 Md. Arch., Prov. Ct., 268. September 26, 10 Md. Arch., Prov. Ct., 293. On June 9 the Governor appointed John Metcalf sheriff of St. Mary's County, 10 Md. Arch., Prov. Ct., 278.
[2] 10 Md. Arch., Prov. Ct., 258.
[3] 10 Md. Arch., Prov. Ct., 260, 293.
[4] 10 Md. Arch., Prov. Ct., 265, 266, 278, 279.
[5] 10 Md. Arch., Prov. Ct., 265, 266, 292.
[6] Wm. Bounday of Patuxent, 10 Md. Arch., Prov. Ct., 271, Cotton, Maryland Calendar of Wills.
[7] John Nunn, 10 Md. Arch., Prov. Ct., 260, 261, 279, 280, 325; Edward Cotton, 277, 345. Nunn, Cotton, and Jas. Knott, in Cotton, Maryland Calendar of Wills.
[8] 10 Md. Arch., Prov. Ct., 272, 276, 280, 339, 340, 366.
[9] 10 Md. Arch., Prov. Ct., 291.
[10] 10 Md. Arch., Prov. Ct., 259, see 160, 185.

tobacco and cask before the end of November. Fortunately for the servant, a third person paid the sum, accepting him as his debtor.

Cattle, of course, were the subject of a number of entries. Earmarks,[1] a gift of a cow,[2] a number of deeds of sale of cows,[3] and an order of court to return a cow which had been lent, are all found.[4] George Rapiar, musician, the first practitioner of the arts known to us in the Province, entered into partnership with John Carrington, planter, giving him a moiety of his five cattle for one thousand two hundred pounds of tobacco and a moiety of his two hundred acres of land, on further condition that Carrington should live with Rapiar for two years "to help to settle and clear" the land.[5] All necessaries bought by either party were to go into the copartnership, and both should be "at equal proportion of charge for all things bought or procured into their family" for housekeeping.

Two entries dealt with land. Cornwallis agreed to transfer to Cornelius Canada, brickmaker, three hundred acres of land on the Patuxent in return for thirty-six thousand "good, sound, well burned bricks." A third of these were to be made that year on the Potomac, or Patuxent, as Cornwallis should appoint, and he must furnish two servants to assist Canada. The remainder of the bricks must be delivered before the end of June, 1654, at the water front of Canada's plantation, "where they may conveniently be fetched away by boat," unless Cornwallis wished them by Christmas, when they should be made on his plantation with the help of his servants. Canada should also pay

---

[1] 10 Md. Arch., Prov. Ct., 260, 293.
[2] 10 Md. Arch., Prov. Ct., 265.
[3] 10 Md. Arch., Prov. Ct., 260, 261, 291, 293, 352.
[4] 10 Md. Arch., Prov. Ct., 277.
[5] 10 Md. Arch., Prov. Ct., 290. Gerard sold Mitchell four heifers with calf or calves at their side, of Gerard's own stock and to be selected out of twelve, at Mitchell's return from England. Mitchell is to choose two and Gerard two. If Mitchell die, the person authorized to demand the cows for his children shall choose one of the cattle, 10 Md. Arch., Prov. Ct., 266. Mitchell filed a power of attorney to two men at this time, 10 Md. Arch., Prov. Ct., 267.

yearly, as a quitrent, five bushels of Indian corn, or twenty shillings sterling. This deed is another proof of the fact that bricks were early made in the Province and in large quantities. The other land record is a suit successfully brought by a planter against Robert Clarke, the Surveyor General,[1] for refusing to survey for him one hundred acres on Draper's Neck, which he claimed by warrant, and for surveying it for Francis Brooke,[2] "upon a more general and subsequent warrant." Brooke was allowed, in lieu of this land, two hundred acres "not yet taken up."

Hatton, the Provincial Secretary,[3] had been "at great charges" for the entertainment of the widow and children of his brother, Richard. The widow afterwards married Lieutenant Richard Banks. In consideration of Hatton's releasing them from all debts touching the above named charges, they assigned to him all right and title to land due to Mrs. Banks for the transportation of herself and her children into Maryland.[4] One of these children, Elinor, whom her father a little before his death had recommended to the care and tuition of Thomas Hatton, was, in 1654, detained by Luke Gardiner at his house in an "uncivil, refractory, insolent manner." Her mother and uncle feared that Gardiner was endeavoring "to train her up in the Roman Catholic religion, contrary to their mind, and often demanded her" of Gardiner, but he refused to return her, "standing upon audacious, peremptory terms." They then complained to Governor Stone, who found this "unsufferable dealing" of Gardiner "not only a great affront to the government and an injury to the girl's mother and uncle, but likewise of very dangerous and destructive consequence in relation to the peace and welfare of this Province." Therefore, he directed Banks, her stepfather, the commander of Newtown Hundred, to take such assistance as might be

---

[1] 10 Md. Arch., Prov. Ct., 270.
[2] Francis Brooke was fined on the next day for profane swearing in court, 10 Md. Arch., Prov. Ct., 276.
[3] 10 Md. Arch., Prov. Ct., 259, see 298. On Hatton see Davis, 200.
[4] 10 Md. Arch., Prov. Ct., 354, 356.

necessary, and using force if needful, to seize Elinor Hatton and to bring her before the Council "to be disposed of as shall be fit," and to arrest Gardiner and bring him also. If she were concealed, Banks was empowered to search Gardiner's house and any other place where he might suspect that he could find her. On April 10, 1654, all parties were brought before the court, and the child was ordered to be returned to her uncle, while no order was made with reference to Gardiner.[1]

In two cases we find that the court allowed the winner not only court charges but also a sum of tobacco for "his trouble and expense in attending the Court."[2] A suit was tried for payment for the "entertainment, with houseroom and diet," of "about 50 servants and storage for goods which came last year in Capt. Richard Husbands' ship."[3] In another case a Virginia judgment is set up and the hearing is respited till the next court, that a copy of the judgment might be procured.[4] Thus early did Maryland give full faith and credit to the judgments of the other colonies. In a third case the plaintiff sued[5] for two barrels of corn, and the "sheriff, on the defendant's behalf," alleged his sickness, desired respite, but "withal attested that the defendant confessed the debt," which was "payable at the Governor's house," and "desired that the corn might be sent for." The Governor, after hearing this rather remarkable speech, agreed, on the defendant's behalf, to satisfy Secretary Hatton, "who was willing to spare the plaintiff" the corn and to hold the defendant responsible for both the corn and the charges. As we hear no more of it, we may fairly surmise that Hatton was duly repaid.

Robert Brooke had certain timber of two men named Ketchmay[6] attached for their failure to provide him with

---

[1] Bozman, II, 492.
[2] 10 Md. Arch., Prov. Ct., 272, 276.
[3] 10 Md. Arch., Prov. Ct., 272.
[4] 10 Md. Arch., Prov. Ct., 270. No further record is found.
[5] 10 Md. Arch., Prov. Ct., 269.
[6] 10 Md. Arch., Prov. Ct., 277, 278, 367; see for a similar case 273. Two or three entries about the payment of sums of tobacco by divers men are found on 278, 279.

casks for his tobacco, because of which he alleged that he was damaged at least three thousand pounds of tobacco, as he had two great houses full of tobacco. One of these houses measured one hundred feet by thirty-two and the other ninety feet by thirty-two, and by long hanging therein much of the tobacco wasted, and a great part of it was blown down and spoiled during the latter end of winter. On April 11, 1654, one of the men had the attachment dissolved, so far as he was concerned, as Brooke had not appeared to make good his claim.

The same George Ketchmay was involved, however, in a very shameful case of adultery, for which the woman concerned was tried at the September court after the birth of an illegitimate child.[1] In April, 1654, she was discharged, as the crime was committed in Virginia, and no proceedings seem ever to have been taken against the man.

PROVINCIAL COURT, OCTOBER, 1653, AND FEBRUARY, 1653/4.

Between October, 1653, and February, 1653/4, we find a number of entries on the court records.[2] Several deeds of sale of cows were entered, especially one of a cow bought by Thomas Hatton from Richard Bennett and transferred to the herd of Mrs. Eure, Baltimore's sister, in return for tobacco received by Hatton from the sale of a bull and a steer sold for the lady at the Proprietary's direction.

Stone recorded a deed of his land[3] in Northampton County, Virginia, to Captain William Whittington, and two other deeds of land appear: one from Cornwallis of a neck of land, containing about one hundred acres, in his manor of Cornwallis Cross, for one thousand five hundred pounds of tobacco and cask and "a very good flitch of bacon," with a quitrent of "half a barrel of good Indian corn and a couple of poultry."

A bond,[4] two releases from debts, a demand from James

---
[1] 10 Md. Arch., Prov. Ct., 272, 276, 280 ff., 339, 340, 366.
[2] 10 Md. Arch., Prov. Ct., 298, 299, 301, 304. Earmarks are also entered, 10 Md. Arch., Prov. Ct., 301, 304, 308.
[3] 10 Md. Arch., Prov. Ct., 298, 300, 305.
[4] 10 Md. Arch., Prov. Ct., 300, 301.

Allen's estate for attendance on the decedent during his sickness,[1] powers of attorney,[2] depositions about the ownership of a sloop,[3] and an agreement to apprentice Blanche Howell for ten years to Thomas Copley and his successors, that is, the Jesuits, who shall not sell her to any other person,[4] are found. There was recorded a remarkable agreement between Thomas Wilford of Virginia and Paul Simpson.[5] In return for twenty thousand pounds of tobacco from Simpson, Wilford agreed to find him, during his life, "sufficient wholesome meat, drink, apparel, both linen and woolen, lodging, washing and other necessaries, well beseeming and fitting a gentleman and, when nails and carpenter can be had, to build him a 15 foot house square with a Welsh chimney, the house to be floored and lofted with deal boards and lined with riven boards on the inside, with a handsome joined bedstead, one small joined table and six joined stools and 3 wainscot chairs, and to furnish the said room with bedding, curtains and valance, chamber linen and all other things fitting and convenient." This room, whose location is not given, should be Simpson's home during his life, and he should be allowed a "servant to get him wood to burn in his chamber and to do him such service" as he shall command. In addition, Wilford agreed to buy for Simpson, "once every year during his life, one anchor of drams, a tierce of sack, and a case of English spirits, to be delivered to him at the time of shipping, for his own spending and drinking."

---

[1] Administration is granted upon the estate of Thomas Balmer of Patuxent, 10 Md. Arch., Prov. Ct., 307. Estates of Walter King, Jas. Allen, and Edward Shelley, in Cotton, Maryland Calendar of Wills.
[2] 10 Md. Arch., Prov. Ct., 303, 307.
[3] 10 Md. Arch., Prov. Ct., 304.
[4] 10 Md. Arch., Prov. Ct., 306.
[5] 10 Md. Arch., Prov. Ct., 302. On page 321 is a curious affidavit by Henry Bishop that John Hammond had given him a letter for Simpson, who was supposed to be in Virginia, and as Bishop did not cross the Potomac after all, he returned the letter to Hammond. Pakes came and Hammond read him the letter, whose contents Bishop has forgotten, and Pakes then asked Hammond what he should do and was answered, "You were best to go yourself to Simpson."

Provincial Court, February, 1653/4.

The Provincial Court sat on three days in February[1] and was much occupied with the estate of John Stringer, carpenter, who died much indebted and whose estate was put in the charge of Rev. William Wilkinson. Mr. Wilkinson preached a funeral sermon, for which and for a funeral dinner he brought in a bill. A number of other creditors filed suits against the estate, the largest of whom, William Allen, merchant, was made administrator. A mortgage of land,[2] a deed of sale of a cow,[3] a deposition concerning the merchantability of certain tobacco, are the only other entries in February, save the suit of John Johnson and Thomas Adams against Colonel Francis Yardley, Nathaniel Batts, and Charles Thurston for the seizure of their vessel in the Potomac River.[4] Yardley answered that he seized the vessel because she came lately from trading at the Dutch plantations, but neither he nor his accomplices in the act proved to the satisfaction of the court that the vessel could be a lawful prize, or that they had any lawful warrant to take her. The ship had been for two months at Accomac, and came to Maryland freighted with cattle belonging to people who lived there. One or both of the owners were inhabitants of Virginia who came up to Maryland with intent to "seat within this Province." None of the Dutch nation had any interest in the vessel, and the court apprehended for "very sufficient reasons that this enterprise was merely undertaken and grounded, upon a malicious quarrel," so the vessel and its contents were ordered to be restored to the plaintiffs and a threefold satisfaction to be paid by Yardley, "who takes the business wholly upon himself," if any goods

---
[1] 10 Md. Arch., Prov. Ct., February (1) 309, (6) 311, (15) 313 (Wm. Waring, formerly a freeman, had covenanted to serve Stringer three years on condition that he be taught the carpenter's trade, and he is now discharged), 328, 330, 333, 352, 360, 361, 369, 379, 384, 395. Estates of Anne Brooks and Thomas Pitts, Cotton, Maryland Calendar of Wills.
[2] 10 Md. Arch., Prov. Ct., 310.
[3] 10 Md. Arch., Prov. Ct., 317.
[4] 10 Md. Arch., Prov. Ct., 312. Batts was Yardley's interpreter, 10 Md. Arch., Prov. Ct., 347.

have been embezzled. Yardley must pay three thousand pounds of tobacco and cask as fine to the Proprietary and also the costs. Batts, "a main instigator and actor in this business," must pay a fine of one thousand pounds of tobacco and cask or receive thirty-nine lashes. Thurston, however, acknowledged his offence, alleged that he was "ignorantly drawn into the attempt, by the Colonel's information that the same was approved of by the Governor and justifiable, and had formerly carried himself unreproveably," so that he was discharged.

PROVINCIAL COURT, MARCH, 1653/4.

A term of court, beginning March 1, 1653/4, lasted for five days.[1] In April the court sat on the tenth and eleventh and again for a short while on the twenty-eighth. On March 6 the record reads that "after the governor and council (present this day) had for some time sat in consultation about some affairs in relation to the public safety, they fell upon hearing of some particular causes." We wonder what the "affairs" were, for the position of the Council was a troublous one; but, as we are ignorant of them, we must turn to the "particular causes."

During these months we find the usual routine business,[2] as if there were no "affairs in relation to the public safety." Earmarks are registered,[3] cattle are sold[4] and their ownership is claimed,[5] powers of attorney are filed,[6] judgments confessed,[7] nonsuits decreed,[8] cases postponed,[9] a testamentary

---
[1] 10 Md. Arch., Prov. Ct., March (1) 321, (2) 325, (3) 332, (4) 338, (6) 346.
[2] 10 Md. Arch., Prov. Ct., 348, 356, 362, 370, 378. Medley asks allowance for his great charge in keeping Robert Greene, request referred to Assembly, 10 Md. Arch., Prov. Ct., 369.
[3] 10 Md. Arch., Prov. Ct., 319, 322, 370, 377.
[4] 10 Md. Arch., Prov. Ct., 318, 319, 320, 351, 355.
[5] 10 Md. Arch., Prov. Ct., 337, 340, 341.
[6] 10 Md. Arch., Prov. Ct., 322, 336 (by Simon Groves of New England, tobacco roller), 347, 352, 356, 357, 358, 367, 368, 370.
[7] 10 Md. Arch., Prov. Ct., 319, 320, 321, 322, 324, 328, 329, 331, 332, 333, 335, 338, 343, 355, 359, 361, 364, 366.
[8] 10 Md. Arch., Prov. Ct., 338, 346, 369, 370.
[9] 10 Md. Arch., Prov. Ct., 328, 332, 334 (cases where the defendant did not appear and therefore postponed), 344, 345, 356, 359, 365, 367.

Appendix.

PROVINCIAL COURT, FEBRUARY, 1653/4.

The Provincial Court sat on three days in February[1] and was much occupied with the estate of John Stringer, carpenter, who died much indebted and whose estate was put in the charge of Rev. William Wilkinson. Mr. Wilkinson preached a funeral sermon, for which and for a funeral dinner he brought in a bill. A number of other creditors filed suits against the estate, the largest of whom, William Allen, merchant, was made administrator. A mortgage of land,[2] a deed of sale of a cow,[3] a deposition concerning the merchantability of certain tobacco, are the only other entries in February, save the suit of John Johnson and Thomas Adams against Colonel Francis Yardley, Nathaniel Batts, and Charles Thurston for the seizure of their vessel in the Potomac River.[4] Yardley answered that he seized the vessel because she came lately from trading at the Dutch plantations, but neither he nor his accomplices in the act proved to the satisfaction of the court that the vessel could be a lawful prize, or that they had any lawful warrant to take her. The ship had been for two months at Accomac, and came to Maryland freighted with cattle belonging to people who lived there. One or both of the owners were inhabitants of Virginia who came up to Maryland with intent to "seat within this Province." None of the Dutch nation had any interest in the vessel, and the court apprehended for "very sufficient reasons that this enterprise was merely undertaken and grounded, upon a malicious quarrel," so the vessel and its contents were ordered to be restored to the plaintiffs and a threefold satisfaction to be paid by Yardley, "who takes the business wholly upon himself," if any goods

---

[1] 10 Md. Arch., Prov. Ct., February (1) 309, (6) 311, (15) 313 (Wm. Waring, formerly a freeman, had covenanted to serve Stringer three years on condition that he be taught the carpenter's trade, and he is now discharged), 328, 330, 333, 352, 360, 361, 369, 379, 384, 395. Estates of Anne Brooks and Thomas Pitts, Cotton, Maryland Calendar of Wills.
[2] 10 Md. Arch., Prov. Ct., 310.
[3] 10 Md. Arch., Prov. Ct., 317.
[4] 10 Md. Arch., Prov. Ct., 312. Batts was Yardley's interpreter, 10 Md. Arch., Prov. Ct., 347.

have been embezzled. Yardley must pay three thousand pounds of tobacco and cask as fine to the Proprietary and also the costs. Batts, "a main instigator and actor in this business," must pay a fine of one thousand pounds of tobacco and cask or receive thirty-nine lashes. Thurston, however, acknowledged his offence, alleged that he was "ignorantly drawn into the attempt, by the Colonel's information that the same was approved of by the Governor and justifiable, and had formerly carried himself unreproveably," so that he was discharged.

Provincial Court, March, 1653/4.

A term of court, beginning March 1, 1653/4, lasted for five days.[1] In April the court sat on the tenth and eleventh and again for a short while on the twenty-eighth. On March 6 the record reads that "after the governor and council (present this day) had for some time sat in consultation about some affairs in relation to the public safety, they fell upon hearing of some particular causes." We wonder what the "affairs" were, for the position of the Council was a troublous one; but, as we are ignorant of them, we must turn to the "particular causes."

During these months we find the usual routine business,[2] as if there were no "affairs in relation to the public safety." Earmarks are registered,[3] cattle are sold[4] and their ownership is claimed,[5] powers of attorney are filed,[6] judgments confessed,[7] nonsuits decreed,[8] cases postponed,[9] a testamentary

---
[1] 10 Md. Arch., Prov. Ct., March (1) 321, (2) 325, (3) 332, (4) 338, (6) 346.
[2] 10 Md. Arch., Prov. Ct., 348, 356, 362, 370, 378. Medley asks allowance for his great charge in keeping Robert Greene, request referred to Assembly, 10 Md. Arch., Prov. Ct., 369.
[3] 10 Md. Arch., Prov. Ct., 319, 322, 370, 377.
[4] 10 Md. Arch., Prov. Ct., 318, 319, 320, 351, 355.
[5] 10 Md. Arch., Prov. Ct., 337, 340, 341.
[6] 10 Md. Arch., Prov. Ct., 322, 336 (by Simon Groves of New England, tobacco roller), 347, 352, 356, 357, 358, 367, 368, 370.
[7] 10 Md. Arch., Prov. Ct., 319, 320, 321, 322, 324, 328, 329, 331, 332, 333, 335, 338, 343, 355, 359, 361, 364, 366.
[8] 10 Md. Arch., Prov. Ct., 338, 346, 369, 370.
[9] 10 Md. Arch., Prov. Ct., 328, 332, 334 (cases where the defendant did not appear and therefore postponed), 344, 345, 356, 359, 365, 367.

matter is determined,[1] a warrant issued,[2] attachments are laid,[3] receipts and releases filed,[4] witness fees allowed,[5] bonds recorded.[6] A charge of bastardy is made.[7] A fugitive servant has her term of service lengthened,[8] a second servant is granted his "clothes, corn, &c" out of his master's estate,[9] a third servant has been lent by Clarke to Boreman and has run away from the latter in Virginia, for which escape recompense is made to Clarke.[10] Richard Moore requests that the line be run between his plantation and that of the children of Anthony Rawlings, for their stepfather, Michael Baisey, molests Moore, threatens to take his land from him and burn his house, and twice refused to let Clarke, the Surveyor, run the line, so that Moore may know what properly is his right and "may live quietly in his last age."[11] The court directs that the survey be perfected, and that, if the Rawlings children have cause of complaint, "they may apply themselves to the Court for relief." Extents are granted in two cases for the value of a debt,[12] in one of which cases, as the land was a manor, three men were appointed to determine how many years the creditor should have the land in payment of his debt.

John Hammond[13] sues Cuthbert Fenwick for damage to his horse and its furniture. He claims that one evening he and his wife, while riding to Patuxent, came to Fenwick's house. The latter asked for the loan of the horse, but was denied, as Hammond expected to return suddenly and so delivered his horse to another to take care of it, until

---
[1] William Stephenson's estate, 10 Md. Arch., Prov. Ct., 332.
[2] 10 Md. Arch., Prov. Ct., 346.
[3] 10 Md. Arch., Prov. Ct., 324, 332, 343, 346, 364, 368, 369.
[4] 10 Md. Arch., Prov. Ct., 349, 350, 352, 353, 356.
[5] 10 Md. Arch., Prov. Ct., 369.
[6] 10 Md. Arch., Prov. Ct., 349. 351 (of Thomas Ringe, a smith), 354. Judgment given for plaintiff, but as he neglected to prosecute, he pays costs, 361.
[7] 10 Md. Arch., Prov. Ct., 337.
[8] 10 Md. Arch., Prov. Ct., 322.
[9] 10 Md. Arch., Prov. Ct., 335, 370.
[10] 10 Md. Arch., Prov. Ct., 331, 335, 366.
[11] 10 Md. Arch., Prov. Ct., 330.
[12] 10 Md. Arch., Prov. Ct., 345, 360.
[13] 10 Md. Arch., Prov. Ct., 339, 367, 386.

his return from the other side of the river. The next morning Fenwick took away the horse and detained it five weeks and four days, in spite of many messages. Finally, he sent it back, detaining a carpet, and with the bridle changed, the saddle torn to pieces, one stirrup, no girth or saddle cloth. He refused to make any satisfaction. As a result of the suit Fenwick is obliged to pay damages and costs.

William Nugent sues Richard Watson for damages received from Watson's not performing his agreement to build a house twenty feet long for Nugent.[1] The defendant denies the bargain and the matter is referred to a jury, which hears testimony and gives the plaintiff a verdict for three hundred pounds of tobacco and costs.

Henry Fox petitions that Philip Land may be ordered to give a speedy account and satisfaction touching their partnership estate, and Land agreeing thereto, the matter is referred to two arbitrators, who might choose an umpire if they could not agree.[2]

Among the numerous cases of these two months are a number in which the payment of debts is demanded.[3] Most of these have but little interest. One of the more interesting ones is the suit of Walter Pakes against John Hammond[4] to recover the purchase money for the plantation which he sold Hammond. The latter alleged certain false pretences and the business was put to arbitration, with

---

[1] 10 Md. Arch., Prov. Ct., 345, 363. On 351 is a curious deposition about a case of strong waters brought by Capt. Husbands from England for Thos. Hatton, but broken open and the contents of the bottles drunk out or spilt on the voyage.

[2] 10 Md. Arch., Prov. Ct., 343.

[3] 10 Md. Arch., Prov. Ct., (1) 323, 381; (2) 331, 276 (Fenwick v. Mitchell, latter sent with tobacco to Holland in March, 1651/2, to give it to Lawrence Coughen, which he never did. Judgment was given); (3) 332; (4) 334, 370, 387; (5) 336; (6) 336, 337, 365; (7) 347, 351 (a parcel of sugar); (8) 341, 366, 385 (suit against Lawrence Starkey, successor to Thos. Copley, deceased); (9) 342; (10) 357; (11) 358 ("a good hog with corn sufficient to feed him withal till he were delivered in Virginia"); (12) 358 ("2 sides of bacon"); (13) 359; (14) 362; (15) 346, 364, 391 (for two voyages from Virginia for Yardley to his plantation in Maryland); (16) 364; (17) 364, 365, 385; (18) 368 (a pair of brass shot moulds); (19) 373 (Giles Brent's bill of 1648).

[4] 10 Md. Arch., Prov. Ct., 344, 385.

Appendix. 153

the consent of both parties, but Hammond delayed so long that Pakes brings suit. Hammond alleges that he had acted as Pakes's attorney in a difference the latter had with Simpson, and that Pakes, in return for this service, remitted the remainder of the purchase price. He cannot prove, however, that he had not rendered his service gratis, and the matter is postponed and settled out of court.

PROVINCIAL COURT, MAY AND JULY, 1654.

The Provincial Court met on May 23 and 24 and on July 16,[1] and the proceedings are as full of routine and as free from signs of impending change as possible. Sales of crops,[2] testamentary matters,[3] bonds,[4] assignments,[5] releases,[6] postponements of hearings,[7] powers of attorney,[8] earmark registry,[9] a gift of cattle for the maintenance of a minister in the neck of Wicocomoco and for the poor and for other pious uses of the parish,[10] a commercial protest,[11] attachments,[12] acknowledgment of debt,[13] or confession of judgment,[14] a few debts,[15]—these are the matters recorded on the eve of Baltimore's loss of the Province. Two fugitive servants were sent back to their master, from whom

---

[1] 10 Md. Arch., Prov. Ct., 382, 383, 391, 396.
[2] 10 Md. Arch., Prov. Ct., 380, 392.
[3] Thomas Copley's estate, 10 Md. Arch., Prov. Ct., 385, Francis Posey's estate 378, 382, John Winbridge's estate 395, Richard Moore's estate 395, 396, 400, 433, 442. July 6, Peter Godson, surgeon, about to marry Moore's widow (Moore was in court on April 10), agreed to lay no claim to Moore's estate, but to leave it to Moore's children. Estate of Geo. Rapiar, 391.
[4] 10 Md. Arch., Prov. Ct., 378, 379.
[5] 10 Md. Arch., Prov. Ct., 379.
[6] 10 Md. Arch., Prov. Ct., 379, 380.
[7] 10 Md. Arch., Prov. Ct., 382, 387.
[8] 10 Md. Arch., Prov. Ct., 382, 388, 397, 398 (Cornwallis, dated July 3).
[9] 10 Md. Arch., Prov. Ct., 393, 394.
[10] 10 Md. Arch., Prov. Ct., 393. Davis, 146.
[11] 10 Md. Arch., Prov. Ct., 394.
[12] 10 Md. Arch., Prov. Ct., 382, 387, 391, 441.
[13] 10 Md. Arch., Prov. Ct., 397.
[14] 10 Md. Arch., Prov. Ct., 387.
[15] 10 Md. Arch., Prov. Ct., 382, 383 (for tobacco and a smoothing iron), 386, 389, 391 (for two anchors of drams to each of two men), 397.

they had run away after correction for just cause,[1] two contracts of service were upheld, as was an indenture which provides for a grant to the servant of fifty acres of land only, without the usual corn or clothes.[2] These things show how important an element in Maryland were the indentured servants.

Provincial Court, October, 1654.

Just before the session of the Assembly, the Provincial Court came together on October 16, 1654, six of the Parliamentary Commissioners being present.[3] There is nothing in the proceedings to show the change of government, but everything is transacted according to the former rules. Dr. Peter Godson acknowledged himself sorry for having accused a woman of being a witch, and paid the charges of a suit against him.[4] Mrs. Godson was also sued for slander, and was bound over for good behavior,[5] and Mrs. Brooke was ordered to pay costs for saying, without being able to prove it, that another woman "had beaten her maid two hours by the clock."[6] There may have been some ground for her charges, however, for on April 24, 1655, a maid-servant, who had run away from the woman accused of cruelty, complained of "extreme usage" and expressed "great fear" of returning to her service, "because of such rigor," so that the court set her free, decreeing that she should lose the corn and clothes she should have received at the expiration of her term of service and should give security to pay her late master "500 lb. tobacco and cask at the first crop ensuing." A collection of six hundred pounds of tobacco was immediately taken up for her in the court.

At this October term another servant successfully complained to the court that his master did not give him suffi-

---
[1] 10 Md. Arch., Prov. Ct., 396.
[2] 10 Md. Arch., Prov. Ct., 356, 379, 381, 382.
[3] 10 Md. Arch., Prov. Ct., 398.
[4] 10 Md. Arch., Prov. Ct., 399.
[5] 10 Md. Arch., Prov. Ct., 402, 403, 409.
[6] 10 Md. Arch., Prov. Ct., 401, 402, 416.

cient clothing,[1] and a third received an order that his master should give him "his corn and clothes," as his term of service had expired.

A man was given a small penalty for assault and battery upon a woman,[2] affidavits were filed concerning the illegal killing of hogs,[3] and concerning thefts by a maid from her mistress. A man successfully maintained his right to a bed which had been given him in England before he came to Maryland as an indentured servant;[4] a non-resident was committed to the sheriff's custody till he should pay a debt or give security for it; a case was referred to the Assembly, as an important party "hath been long absent and is to be present" then;[5] and a man recorded a deed of a two-year-old heifer to his daughter in exchange for five hogs.[6]

Dr. Peter Godson demanded one thousand four hundred and thirty pounds of tobacco from the husband of one of his patients "for physic and surgery," and expert testimony having been used for the first time in the Province, the account[7] was "examined by men of the same faculty and regulated to 590 lbs. tobacco," for which account judgment was given. Mr. Preston, the new Secretary, was empowered to hear a suit for debt, in which the defendant could not appear at the court, "through infirmities of body." If sufficient answer should not be shown Preston within a fortnight, execution should issue upon the bill.[8]

A man was ordered to give security to deliver another man four rights of land due him.[9] Francis Brooke was ordered to pay costs of a suit brought against him by Isaac Ilvie of Kent Island, who charged that his possession of

---

[1] 10 Md. Arch., Prov. Ct., 401, 406.
[2] 10 Md. Arch., Prov. Ct., 400, 401, 404, 422. For miscellaneous entries: subpoena 405, postponement 405, acknowledgment 404, witness fees 401, 403, nonsuits 403, 404.
[3] 10 Md. Arch., Prov. Ct., 402.
[4] 10 Md. Arch., Prov. Ct., 403.
[5] 10 Md. Arch., Prov. Ct., 404.
[6] 10 Md. Arch., Prov. Ct., 406. Earmarks filed on same page.
[7] 10 Md. Arch., Prov. Ct., 399.
[8] 10 Md. Arch., Prov. Ct., 401. For another contract case see 403.
[9] 10 Md. Arch., Prov. Ct., 401.

two hundred acres, called Beaver Neck, was disturbed by Brooke, pretending a grant from Baltimore and power from the Governor, which do not appear.[1] Philip Connors, the commander of the Isle of Kent, was directed to cause the sheriff to give Ilvie quiet possession of his land. John Hambleton demanded a sum of tobacco from Fenwick, who replied that the debt was paid by a sale of land he had made Hambleton, but the latter did not acknowledge the bargain; after some debate in court, the parties agreed to refer the whole matter to "the arbitration of two indifferent men."[2]

Two estates of decedents came before the court,[3] one of them owing a number of debts, among which were charges for physic in the time of the man's sickness and for "his winding sheet and burying of his corpse."

COURT BUSINESS, DECEMBER, 1654, TO APRIL, 1655.

The only winter session of the Provincial Court occurred[4] on December 5, 1654, when five Commissioners, headed by Preston, were present. The proceedings contain little of interest. Constables were appointed, and John Hammond, who had agreed to build at his own cost a suitable court-house for "St. Mary's and Potomac Counties" alongside of his house as the most convenient place for the "keeping of courts," was granted, in return for his public spirit, license to retail wine and strong liquors and to keep a "ferry for the convenient passage of people over Newtown River."[5] A woman failed to prove a charge of rape, and the same woman's husband failed in proving a charge of some sort against another woman with whom his wife had quar-

---
[1] 10 Md. Arch., Prov. Ct., 404.
[2] A man was ordered to pay for damages his wife had occasioned her former master, 10 Md. Arch., Prov. Ct., 405.
[3] Thomas Connery, 10 Md. Arch., Prov. Ct., 406, 449, Thomas Trumpeter, 398, 399, 400, 401. Thomas Harris and William Jones, Cotton, Maryland Calendar of Wills.
[4] 10 Md. Arch., Prov. Ct., 407.
[5] 10 Md. Arch., Prov. Ct., 410; witness fees, 407, 408, 409; postponements, 407–410; earmarks, 412; bond, 408, 412; crop sales, 412; power of attorney, 408; rights to land, 407, 408, 409, 410; attachments, 407, 410; confession of judgment, 407.

Appendix. 157

reled.[1] A few cases of debt,[2] one entry allowing Preston a sum out of the Provincial levy in return for his paying a bill,[3] and the care of the estate of Samuel Griffin[4] complete the court business at this time.

The most important business of the April court was the trial of various persons for acts committed during the war of 1654. Other business was of a routine character. Several estates of decedents were brought before it,[5] one being Cuthbert Fenwick's, and another that of Thomas Hebden, who had died several years previously, leaving all his property to his wife by will, but making a deed of trust of certain property for the use of the Jesuits, concerning which property certain difficulties had arisen with Mrs. Hebden, but were now settled. Mrs. Hebden seems to have practiced medicine, and recovered a sum for "physic charges."[6]

PROVINCIAL COURT, JUNE TO SEPTEMBER, 1655.

When the Provincial Court met at Patuxent, on June 26, 1655, five Commissioners were present. Thomas Mears and Thomas Marsh were added as Commissioners, since " the attendance of divers members of this court is taken off and by reason of their several occasions and employments calling them at present out of the Province."[7] On August 13 six members were present, and Captain Sampson

---

[1] 10 Md. Arch., Prov. Ct., 407, 408, 409, 411.
[2] 10 Md. Arch., Prov. Ct., 408, 415. Security given, 407, 408, 409, 411. Nonsuit, 408, 409, 410.
[3] 10 Md. Arch., Prov. Ct., 409.
[4] 10 Md. Arch., Prov. Ct., 409, 410, 414, 433, 450.
[5] 10 Md. Arch., Prov. Ct., Cuthbert Fenwick 413, 431, 451, 473, George Dolt 415, Jas. Memeis 415, Thomas Hebden 46, 418, 4 Md. Arch., Prov. Ct., 512. Attachments, 10 Md. Arch., Prov. Ct., 417. Debts 414 (Cornwallis), 415, 416, 417 (for a boat borrowed). Estates of Ralph Beane, John Hodges, Mrs. Peter Godson, Richard Lawrence, in Cotton, Maryland Calendar of Wills. Witness fees, 10 Md. Arch., Prov. Ct., 416, servant's corn and clothes 415.
[6] 10 Md. Arch., Prov. Ct., 415, 422.
[7] 3 Md. Arch., Coun., 316; 10 Md. Arch., Prov. Ct., 419. The court made a decree with reference to a contract to make tobacco hogsheads; and later an attachment was granted upon the order, 10 Md. Arch., Prov. Ct., 449.

158   *Maryland Under the Commonwealth.*

Waring, Michael Brooke, John Pott,[1] and Woodman Stockley were "added" to the number of Provincial Commissioners. Leonard Strong, merchant, had gone to England,[2] to publish "Babylon's Fall" and to die, and the remaining Commissioners assumed the right to add to their number from time to time. In the records for August 13 we find Fuller is styled Governor. On that day an order was made for the captains of the trainbands of Patuxent to summon all the people forth for military exercise. Those not appearing should be fined and disarmed if obstinate. The public arms lent to individuals must be returned, unless in the possession of persons "well affected to the present government" and "fit to be confided in."

On August 22 the court met again,[3] five Commissioners being present and Fuller presiding. The sheriff was given power to distrain the goods of such persons as should refuse to pay public dues, and a bond is recorded, as is a deed of gift of bedding, a fowling-piece, and an iron pot from a woman about to marry again to the son of her first husband.

In October a more important three-day term of court was held,[4] and the court came together again for one day late in December. Fuller was not present at this last court, and his frequent absences show that he was regarded as President of the Commissioners, rather than as Governor. A man who had killed another's sow was ordered to replace her with one of like value.[5] Dandy's wife was forced to apologize to one John Milam for scandalizing him by saying, "You would hang up men at the yard's arm, for there

---
[1] 3 Md. Arch., Coun., 317, says Robert Pott.
[2] 10 Md. Arch., Prov. Ct., 440.
[3] 10 Md. Arch., Prov. Ct., 419.
[4] 10 Md. Arch., Prov. Ct., October (3) 420, (5) 423, (8) 428, December 26, 430; earmark recorded 437, nonsuits 429, 435, postponements 429, 435, powers of attorney 430, 433, discharge of debts 421, confession of judgment 422, attachments 427, bonds 424, 430, 436, 437 (two, one by Starkey for goods bought with itemized bill, and one by Job Chandler to a London merchant for 1100 muskrat skins), 438 (Sir Henry Chicheley to Cornwallis), grant of land 432, debts 428, 429, 431, 433-436.
[5] 10 Md. Arch., Prov. Ct., 420, 421; for title to hogs see 433.

Appendix. 159

is no law in the country." He was obliged to "acknowledge his miscarriage" and pay court charges for arresting her for felony without proof. Milam was a merchant, and Dandy was ordered to pay him for goods stolen from Milam's store by one of Dandy's servants. Several testamentary matters were determined, the estate of one man in particular, John Crabtree, causing considerable trouble.[1] Smith, the muster master general, also died, and the sheriffs were directed to collect and pay his widow the four pounds of tobacco per poll directed to be paid him by act of Assembly. A man-servant,[2] who "last served the public," was "allowed his corn and clothes from the public account of fines," and two others were seized and sold to pay a fine to the public owed by their master.[3] Two men were accused of using threatening language, and one of them was fined therefor and for swearing.[4]

One of the medical profession was in bad odor at these courts. Godson was convicted of stealing a bodkin and concealing it, and was made to restore its value fourfold and pay costs. He was also charged by Peter Sharp, chirurgeon, of killing Captain Smith "by taking too much blood from him."[5] The matter was referred to the next court, "when men of skill and ability shall judge of the action," but we hear no more of it. In a third case a man complained that he had paid Godson tobacco for a cure, but the latter "left him worse than he found him."[6] The court ordered him to make a cure or repay the tobacco, and as he failed in the former, he was forced to return the tobacco.

The aftermath of the war is seen in the court records in these months. Stone's estate in Patuxent had been sequestrated and put into William Dorrington's hands to look to,

---

[1] 10 Md. Arch., Prov. Ct., 420-424, 431, 438, 453, 469, 474, 478, 485, John Ramsay's estate 422, John Smith's estate 432, 440, 441, 452.
[2] 10 Md. Arch., Prov. Ct., 431, 433, 436.
[3] For servants see 10 Md. Arch., Prov. Ct., 432, 434 (corn and clothes come after the master's debts to the public are paid).
[4] 10 Md. Arch., Prov. Ct., 421-423.
[5] 10 Md. Arch., Prov. Ct., 424, 432.
[6] 10 Md. Arch., Prov. Ct., 434, 439.

till it should satisfy "the public damage upon his late rebellion,"[1] and in October, Dorrington is cautioned to see that nothing be carried away and is directed to "require aid and assistance to suppress any such riot, or force, and to repell it," if "any should come by force to disturb" him in the possession of the estate. Stone was out of the Province and had no attorney in Maryland, so when John Sutton and Peter Johnson sued him because of false imprisonment for eighteen days, they were granted attachments on Stone's goods.[2] Other attachments[3] were laid on Stone's estate to pay Peter Sharp for "divers arms and provisions" taken from his house by Stone's soldiers and to pay the claims of four other men, one of whom furnished five guns. Preston, another of them, claimed that Fendall had taken guns, etc., from his house.

James Berry was "convicted of several subscriptions against the present government, tending to set up and abet a false and usurped power" of Captain Stone, and was fined the usual two thousand pounds of tobacco, but half of the fine was remitted.[4]

Robert Taylor was convicted of subscribing to a petition against the Puritan government, and was fined one thousand pounds of tobacco,[5] while William Bramhall, who had been convicted, probably by the Anne Arundel County court, of signing "a rebellious petition," had signed another such petition and was ordered to be at the charge of building a pair of stocks within a month.[6] At some time or other Captain John Price had been fined thirty thousand pounds of tobacco, "in relation to his rebellion with Captain Stone," and he pleaded[7] that he was "ancient" and his estate not able to pay the said fine, which was thereupon reduced to

---
[1] 10 Md. Arch., Prov. Ct., 422.
[2] 10 Md. Arch., Prov. Ct., 423, 424.
[3] 10 Md. Arch., Prov. Ct., 425-427, 433.
[4] 10 Md. Arch., Prov. Ct., 423-425.
[5] 10 Md. Arch., Prov. Ct., 424, 425.
[6] 10 Md. Arch., Prov. Ct., 424.
[7] 10 Md. Arch., Prov. Ct., 425. Thos. Trueman had been fined five thousand pounds, 433.

ten thousand pounds, as Owen James's was reduced from five thousand to three thousand pounds[1] and Henry Parnell's from five thousand to four thousand pounds.[2] Job Chandler had been fined fifteen thousand pounds of tobacco,[3] and William Ewen's fine of two thousand pounds was reduced one half.[4] John Jarboe and James Langworth had acted with Captain Stone "in the late Rebellion" unwillingly, and were fined only one thousand pounds of tobacco each.[5]

A number of men openly in court confessed themselves to be Roman Catholics. Of these Lieutenant William Evans seems to have been fined three thousand three hundred pounds of tobacco;[6] Robert Clarke, ten thousand pounds;[7] Thomas Matthews had merely to give surety for his good conduct;[8] William Boreman had his "public offence" remitted, as he submitted "himself to the mercy of the Court," but was fined one thousand pounds of tobacco "towards the damage sustained" by reason of the rebellion;[9] John Dandy also threw himself on the mercy of the court, and was fined two thousand pounds, but had eleven guns and ten locks returned to him;[10] John Pile seems to have suffered nothing.[11]

Mr. Batten's servant, taken captive by Stone and his men, was ordered to be restored to his master.[12] In December a petition of John Norwood, sheriff of Providence, was

---

[1] 10 Md. Arch., Prov. Ct., 426.
[2] 10 Md. Arch., Prov. Ct., 428.
[3] 10 Md. Arch., Prov. Ct., 428.
[4] 10 Md. Arch., Prov. Ct., 429.
[5] 10 Md. Arch., Prov. Ct., 429.
[6] 10 Md. Arch., Prov. Ct., 423, 424.
[7] 10 Md. Arch., Prov. Ct., 425, 426. He turned over a plantation in part payment of the fine, but in March, 1655/6, it was returned to him, as he had no other means of subsistence for himself and his children. If he should ever sell it, half the proceeds must be paid the Province, 441. Later the court remitted Clarke's fine to the public, provided he pay the sheriffs' fees, 534, 558.
[8] 10 Md. Arch., Prov. Ct., 426.
[9] 10 Md. Arch., Prov. Ct., 427.
[10] 10 Md. Arch., Prov. Ct., 429.
[11] 10 Md. Arch., Prov. Ct., 429.
[12] 10 Md. Arch., Prov. Ct., 426.

granted that he might distrain upon the estates of several who were indebted for charges while they were his prisoners after the battle of the Severn.[1]

PROVINCIAL COURT, 1656 TO MAY, 1657.

On the very last day of December, 1655, Sampson Waring gave bond as sheriff and James Veitch as deputy sheriff of the counties of Patuxent, St. Mary's, and Potomac.[2] No session of the court was held until March 20, 1655/6, when four Commissioners met, Fuller presiding.[3] The court met again on April 10 with four Commissioners under Preston's presidency.[4] The sixteenth of June saw the next session with Preston in the chair.[5] An autumn session of four days was held in September, at which Fuller was present,[6] and a second one in October, at which Preston presided.[7] During the winter a court was held in January with Preston as president[8] and one in March, 1656/7, partly under the same presidency[9] and partly under Fuller's. A later session, of unknown date, was held, with seven Commissioners present, under Fuller's presidency,[10] and one met in May under Preston's presidency.[11] During all this period of a year and a half the Provincial Court records are our only source of information as to conditions in the Province. In this time the estates of a number of deceased persons, some of whom were of considerable importance, came before the court,[12] and the usual routine went on. There was little to

---

[1] 10 Md. Arch., Prov. Ct., 430. Wm. Evans, Thos. Trueman, Wm. Stone, Job Chandler, Ed. Packer, Geo. Thompson, Robert Clarke, Henry William, Jno. Cosey. See 435 for order of execution against all who shall refuse or delay to pay public fines.
[2] 3 Md. Arch., Coun., 318; 10 Md. Arch., Prov. Ct., 435, 436.
[3] 10 Md. Arch., Prov. Ct., March (20) 438, (21) 439, (22) 441.
[4] 10 Md. Arch., Prov. Ct., 445.
[5] 10 Md. Arch., Prov. Ct., June (16) 448, (17) 451.
[6] 10 Md. Arch., Prov. Ct., September (22) 456, (23) 459, (24) 461, (25) 463.
[7] 10 Md. Arch., Prov. Ct., October (20) 466, (21) 467.
[8] 10 Md. Arch., Prov. Ct., January (12) 472, (13) 474.
[9] 10 Md. Arch., Prov. Ct., March (10) 481, (20) 486, (21) 488.
[10] 10 Md. Arch., Prov. Ct., 492.
[11] 10 Md. Arch., Prov. Ct., May (14) 499, (15) 504.
[12] Francis Vandan 438, 450, 454, 462, 463, Peter Johnson 439, Ben-

Appendix. 163

distinguish the court in the Puritan days from the same body in the time when the Proprietary's power was recognized. The bulk of the business is made up of the registration of earmarks,[1] of gift,[2] mortgage,[3] or sale of cattle,[4] of suits on ground of unfulfilled contracts and unpaid debts,[5] or those paid in rotten tobacco,[6] of the filing of bonds and mortgages,[7] receipts and discharges,[8] protests,[9] and powers of attorney.[10] Many orders of postponements,[11] allowances for witness fees,[12] and judgments of non-suit[13] are found. Numerous attachments are laid.[14]

On March 21, 1655/6, as Durand was absent from the Province upon urgent occasion,[15] the Commissioners appointed Preston their Secretary. He had a miscellaneous lot

jamin Gill 441, 450, William Edie 441, John Preuce 441, John Norman 451, George Willard 452, William Nugent 453, John Barriff 458, 459, 463, 466, 467 (December, 1657), Friendship Tongue 473, Andrew Scott 479, 494, Thomas Ayer 479, 494, Edward Beasley 479, 483, William Gibbins 480, 482, 485, Thomas Marsh 486, Father Lawrence Starkey 489 (administration given to the greatest creditor), William Eltonhead 503, 523, 553, John Pritchard 505, 551, 552 (Rev. Wm. Wilkinson obtained the residue of the estate for the maintenance of Pritchard's child in January, 1657/8), Thomas Hatton and wife 510, 551, 557, 558, Valerius Leo 483, Andrew Hanson 487.

[1] 10 Md. Arch., Prov. Ct., 444, 472, 482, 491.
[2] 10 Md. Arch., Prov. Ct., 447, 448, 456, 470, 485, 486, 495.
[3] 10 Md. Arch., Prov. Ct., 453, 454.
[4] 10 Md. Arch., Prov. Ct., 498.
[5] 10 Md. Arch., Prov. Ct., 438, 440, 441, 445, 446, 448, 449, 458, 459, 467-469, 471, 473, 475, 476, 478, 480 (a jury trial), 481, 483, 489, 493, 495 (the "Jew's" Store, the first reference to that race in the Province, probably refers to David Farrera, merchant), 482, 489, 490, 491, 498, 500, 501, 504, 509.
[6] 10 Md. Arch., Prov. Ct., 462, 475.
[7] 10 Md. Arch., Prov. Ct., 446, 447, 474, 480, 491, 497, 510, 511.
[8] 10 Md. Arch., Prov. Ct., 442, 447, 479, 497, 498.
[9] 10 Md. Arch., Prov. Ct., 442, 443.
[10] 10 Md. Arch., Prov. Ct., 443-446, 449, 453, 455, 456, 472.
[11] 10 Md. Arch., Prov. Ct., 445, 449-452, 455, 460-463, 466, 468, 476, 479, 483, 494.
[12] 10 Md. Arch., Prov. Ct., 451, 453, 474, 475, 487, 488.
[13] 10 Md. Arch., Prov. Ct., 439-442, 450, 451, 459, 460, 470, 476, 478, 479, 483, 491, 494, 496, 501, 502, 504, 506.
[14] 10 Md. Arch., Prov. Ct., 440, 445, 449 (negro mentioned 461), 492, 500, 503; especially Seamer v. Billingsley, 476, 502, 521-523, case finally referred to arbitrators and decided by them September, 1657. See also Bagby v. Morley, 438, 448, 449, 458.
[15] 10 Md. Arch., Prov. Ct., 442.

of matters to record, interspersing deeds[1] and suits concerning land with questions referred to arbitration,[2] questions as to title to cattle,[3] questions as to the condition and building of housing and fencing.[4] A ferryman is ordered to be paid out of the public levies for transporting people over the Patuxent,[5] a list of the inhabitants in Patuxent and Potomac Counties is directed to be taken,[6] a charge is laid of killing a steer wrongfully,[7] a sheriff is fined for not summoning a defendant,[8] and his bondsman's heirs are freed from the obligation of their security.[9] Maryland hogsheads were larger than those from Virginia, which produced difficulties, and a standard gauge of "43 inches in length and 26 inches over the head" was established.[10]

In the spring of 1657, as the number of Commissioners was small, owing to death and absence, they added to their body six more, namely, Captain Philip Morgan, Mr. William Ewens, Mr. Thomas Thomas, Lieutenant Philip Thomas, Mr. Samuel Vethers, and Lieutenant Richard Woolman.[11]

One accusation of theft[12] is mentioned, and a woman is accused of murdering her infant, but is freed because a jury of eleven women "searched" her body and gave verdict that "she hath not had any child within the time charged."[13] Francis Brooke, who had bought his wife from Captain Mitchell, was charged with beating her so cruelly, while she was pregnant, that she brought forth a dead child, but Brooke went scot free for some reason.[14] A woman accused her husband of abusing and defaming her, but was proved to have defamed him and to be pregnant, though she

---

[1] 10 Md. Arch., Prov. Ct., 443, 460. An assignment of a debt, 497.
[2] 10 Md. Arch., Prov. Ct., 441, 449.
[3] 10 Md. Arch., Prov. Ct., 452, a jury trial 465, 466, 470.
[4] 10 Md. Arch., Prov. Ct., 459, 476.
[5] 10 Md. Arch., Prov. Ct., 470.
[6] 10 Md. Arch., Prov. Ct., 470.
[7] 10 Md. Arch., Prov. Ct., 484, see 493.
[8] 10 Md. Arch., Prov. Ct., 488.
[9] 10 Md. Arch., Prov. Ct., 491.
[10] 10 Md. Arch., Prov. Ct., 492.
[11] 10 Md. Arch., Prov. Ct., 493.
[12] 10 Md. Arch., Prov. Ct., 439, but see 478.
[13] 10 Md. Arch., Prov. Ct., 456.
[14] 10 Md. Arch., Prov. Ct., 464, 466, 488.

had not lived with him for a long time.[1] Her suit was lost sight of, and in January, 1657/8, she was accused of abortion. Another case of adultery[2] was tried, in which a sentence was passed upon each of the defendants of twenty lashes, but the man's punishment was changed to a fine of five hundred pounds of tobacco, at the petition of "divers neighbors."

There were a number of cases involving slander and defamation of character. One who scandalously abused his master and confessed it received ten lashes.[3] A woman, guilty of slandering two other women by accusing them of theft, was committed till she acknowledge in open court that she had done them wrong and "put in security for her good behaviour."[4]

A man accused two others of being forsworn,[5] was ordered to ask them forgiveness in the face of the court and to pay a fine, which latter penalty was afterwards remitted. Another had aspersed the moral character of a man, his wife, and their son, and was condemned to be fined and to stand stripped from the waist upward by the whipping post and to give security for good behavior.[6] He was also charged with slandering a woman by accusing her of unchastity, but the conclusion of that suit has not been found.[7] In still another case the defendant took an appeal from the Kent court, but did not appear to prosecute and was fined for his failure to come.[8]

A separation a mensa et thoro, the first Maryland divorce, was granted to Cornelius Cannady and his wife on June 21,

---

[1] 10 Md. Arch., Prov. Ct., 501, 503, 504, 519, 555 (she was searched by a jury of women).
[2] 10 Md. Arch., Prov. Ct., 506, 521, 556, 558, 560.
[3] 10 Md. Arch., Prov. Ct., 439.
[4] 10 Md. Arch., Prov. Ct., 473, 478.
[5] 10 Md. Arch., Prov. Ct., 475, 478, 481, 483, 491, 502.
[6] 10 Md. Arch., Prov. Ct., 487, 488, 519, 555, 560. Is Matthew Smith's affidavit on 494 a slander?
[7] 10 Md. Arch., Prov. Ct., 495, 528, 555, 560. He accused her of undue intimacy with his Indian servant, and had said, if the servant's "oath could be taken in court, that he could say more in the same business."
[8] 10 Md. Arch., Prov. Ct., 493.

1656, after two men had vainly endeavored to reconcile them.[1]

Dr. Peter Sharp sued a man for seduction of his stepdaughter.[2] The young woman swore that she would not marry the man; but finally, as the defendant claimed that she had promised to marry him, a most curious agreement was drawn up between the parties. Sharp and his wife were unwilling to have the young people marry, but would consent if the woman cared to marry the man, so it was decided that, within fifteen days of the agreement, she was to be "conveyed to a house at the Cliffs and remain there for six weeks, during which time the defendant might have all freedom of discourse with her" provided he brought "one or more of the neighbors with him," and might "use all fair and lawful endeavors with her to marry." One or more of the neighbors must always be present when the defendant was in company with her, and he must pay for "her entertainment" during the whole time. Sharp agreed to put no hinderance in the way of the defendant's success, but to permit the marriage if his stepdaughter wished it. If she were not induced to agree to marry her lover within the six weeks, the latter agreed, "totally and absolutely," to discharge her from any former promise, and never afterwards "endeavor to gain the affection" of the young woman "or to procure any familiarity or discourse with her, or willingly to come into her company." If he married her, he promised that he would not "upbraid, or deride, or any other way exercise, or use any bitterness" to her for "any former passages between them," on penalty of becoming " incapable of intermeddling with or disposing of her estate." The former action was to be withdrawn, the defendant paying his own charges, and also the plaintiff's, if he won his bride; but if he lost her, Dr. Sharp was to charge these to the account of the stepdaughter. One wonders whether she married her lover or not?

---

[1] 10 Md. Arch., Prov. Ct., 449, 471. The name is probably the same as Kennedy.
[2] 10 Md. Arch., Prov. Ct., 499, 531.

Servants as usual occupied much of the court's attention. Two men, alleged to have escaped from Claiborne in Virginia, were ordered to be returned to him by the sheriff, who should press boat and men for that purpose.[1] Captain Mitchell gave bond[2] not to sell a maid-servant for the present,[3] as she swore he had brought her over to serve his children, and had promised that he would not sell her. There are suits concerning the length of service remaining unperformed,[4] the responsibility of paying the expenses of a sick servant,[5] and the payment of freedom-corn and freedom-clothes, which were dismissed.[6] We also find hired servants, who brought suits for wages,[7] and cruel masters who maltreated servants[8] and made them work on the Sabbath day.

Two sets of runaway servants were caught and brought before the court. They seem to have tried to get away to the Swedes in Delaware. The disposition of the first group of men is not stated, but three of the four prisoners in the latter group were whipped, while the fourth, who did not run away but was privy to the plans, was ordered to whip two of the three.[9]

Provincial Court, June to August, 1657.

During this period the Provincial Court continued to meet at Preston's house at Patuxent, and an Assembly was convened. Sessions of the court were held during the sum-

---

[1] 10 Md. Arch., Prov. Ct., 442.
[2] 10 Md. Arch., Prov. Ct., 442.
[3] 10 Md. Arch., Prov. Ct., 445, 446, 451, 463. Mitchell seems to have disposed of her after all, and to have tried to get her back again. He did recover another servant sold contrary to his orders by his agent, see 494, 496.
[4] 10 Md. Arch., Prov. Ct., 451, 472, 494–496.
[5] 10 Md. Arch., Prov. Ct., 452.
[6] 10 Md. Arch., Prov. Ct., 505.
[7] 10 Md. Arch., Prov. Ct., 473, 491, 496, 502, employer was to cure servant of a disease and give him one thousand pounds of tobacco and cask, a kersey or broadcloth suit, two shirts, two pairs of stockings, three pairs of shoes, and a barrel of corn or one hundred pounds of tobacco for a year's service, during which time the servant should also receive diet and lodging.
[8] 10 Md. Arch., Prov. Ct., 474, 482, 484, 488.
[9] 10 Md. Arch., Prov. Ct., 504, 511.

mer of 1657: on June 16, July 25, and August 17 and 22, at all of which Preston presided, with three or four other Commissioners as assessors. In addition to the usual records of sale and gift of cattle,[1] there is one testamentary matter[2] and a deed of land.[3] Two servants[4] were accused of forging a pass and were adjudged to receive twenty lashes apiece. One of them begged for pardon, and on motion of his accuser and upon promise of future good behavior his punishment was remitted, if he would whip his fellow criminal. A deposition was filed accusing a man of bastardy.[5] Against a woman who had left her husband in Virginia and had come to Maryland, where she lived in adultery, a penalty was decreed of twenty lashes upon the bare back, ten immediately at the court door and ten at the river side of Potomac.[6] The sheriff was ordered to deliver her on the Virginia side of the river to the officers there. The man with whom she lived in Maryland broke prison, ran away, and thus escaped punishment. Two fugitive servants were also ordered to be delivered by the sheriff into the custody of the Virginia officers, and he was "empowered to press boat and men to transport them over Potomac."[7]

Provincial Court, September, 1657, to February, 1657/8.

The most important business before the Provincial Court at this September session was the trial and conviction of John Dandy the smith,[8] an old-time offender, for the murder of his servant Henry Gouge. On July 7 Gouge's naked

---

[1] 10 Md. Arch., Prov. Ct., 514, 515, 517.
[2] 10 Md. Arch., Prov. Ct., 514, 519, Richard Harris's estate. His wife filed a caveat in June for administration and was appointed administratrix in September.
[3] Land situated in Virginia, but deed executed at Patuxent in 1655, 10 Md. Arch., Prov. Ct., 518.
[4] 10 Md. Arch., Prov. Ct., 517.
[5] 10 Md. Arch., Prov. Ct., 516. In January, 1657/8, the woman received thirty lashes for her wrong-doing.
[6] 10 Md. Arch., Prov. Ct., 515, 516.
[7] 10 Md. Arch., Prov. Ct., 515.
[8] 10 Md. Arch., Prov. Ct., 522, 524, 525, 534, 542, 546, 557.

body was found in the creek and clearly had not been drowned. Dandy had treated the servant cruelly, having inflicted a serious wound on his head with an axe some time previously, and the last time Gouge was known to be alive was when Dandy had been heard beating him at Dandy's charcoal kiln on the day before the body was found. When Dandy helped to turn the corpse, the old wound on the head and the nose bled, which was supposed to point out the murderer. The servant's clothes were never found. Dandy was arrested on August 7, but fled to Virginia, whence he was returned a week later. He claimed that he fled " to put himself into the custody of some in authority there, that there he might have his trial," for the government of Maryland " is not settled," and he had received hard usage from those in authority in the Province. A coroner's jury of eleven men, being as many of the neighbors as could be conveniently procured, was impanelled and sent with the sheriff and two chirurgeons[1] to disinter Gouge's body and try to determine the cause of death, but they made return that, owing to the decomposed condition of the body, they could make no report. Lieutenant Richard Smith was appointed Attorney General, and a special grand jury of twenty-four men brought in an indictment. On the next day, September 30, a jury was selected,[2] and after hearing the evidence, it brought in a verdict of guilty. The court thereupon sentenced Dandy to be hanged on Saturday, October 3, " upon the island at the mouth of Leonard's Creek in Patuxent River."

Two days before his death, his wife, Anne, petitioned the court that she might not be " left utterly destitute of competent subsistence "[3] for herself and her children, as Dandy's estate was forfeited " to his Highness the Lord Protector " by the conviction. The court seriously considered the matter, and ordered that after the sheriff had taken an inventory of the estate, she should remain possessed of it,

---

[1] Richard Maddox and Emperor Smith. They were allowed a hogshead of tobacco between them as a fee.
[2] Dandy objected to one man and another was substituted.
[3] 10 Md. Arch., Prov. Ct., 546.

170   *Maryland Under the Commonwealth.*

provided that she pay out of it all charges and debts and give security " to give an account and be responsible for the overplus of the said estate," if called upon to do so.

Suits[1] for debt were entered by two men against Dandy on the same day, and Dandy's security on a previous suit asked to be released. On Monday, after the hanging, the court allowed the accounts of the Attorney General, sheriff, and clerk of court, of the man who provided diet for the prisoner and the juries, and of the man who guarded Dandy in Virginia and returned him to Maryland.[2] Later, accounts were allowed of the man who guarded Dandy during the trial.[3] Mrs. Dandy did not give security to be responsible for the estate, but was accused of having " embezzled and carried away " some part of it. The court therefore ordered the sheriff to secure the estate, seize anything that Mrs. Dandy might have carried away wrongfully, and bring her before the next Provincial Court. Dr. Maddox soon married Mrs. Dandy, and on January 1, 1657/8, was ordered to account for the estate.

At the September court we also find the usual number of cases of contract, several of them arising from the staple tobacco.[4] Some of the suits were brought against the estates of men who had died.[5] One deed of a cow,[6] a reconciliation,[7] a receipt,[8] a number of nonsuits,[9] postponements,[10] an acknowledgment,[11] a case of bastardy,[12] one of

---

[1] 10 Md. Arch., Prov. Ct., 545, 546, 548.
[2] 10 Md. Arch., Prov. Ct., 547.
[3] 10 Md. Arch., Prov. Ct., 557 (two debts were claimed at that time, 10 Md. Arch., Prov. Ct., 558, 559), see 553.
[4] 10 Md. Arch., Prov. Ct., 520-522, 525-527, 529-531, 553 (Mrs. Eltonhead; see Mrs. Anne Johnson's deed of gift on second marriage in Cotton, Maryland Calendar of Wills).
[5] 10 Md. Arch., Prov. Ct., Bartholomew Bloom, 534, 554; William Walworth, 520.
[6] 10 Md. Arch., Prov. Ct., 548.
[7] 10 Md. Arch., Prov. Ct., 522.
[8] 10 Md. Arch., Prov. Ct., 548.
[9] 10 Md. Arch., Prov. Ct., 521, 527, 528 (the court adjudged that the plaintiff had no cause of suit, and that the defendant " have in his recullisance wherein he was bound to appear, with cost of suit "), 529, 545.
[10] 10 Md. Arch., Prov. Ct., 522, 527.
[11] 10 Md. Arch., Prov. Ct., 528.
[12] 10 Md. Arch., Prov. Ct., 526.

slander,[1] and one of trespass on the case for the loss of a cow,[2]—such were the matters brought up for consideration. Full faith and credit were given to a Jamestown judgment, and execution was ordered upon it.[3] Servants gave rise to several cases. One man complained that the overseer "did inhumanly beat him" and exact that the servants should "beat their victuals," i. e., pound corn, in the night, and "that they often times want victuals."[4] The court ordered that the overseer forbear to beat the servant unlawfully, do not exact that he beat corn in the night-time, and provide sufficient diet for all the servants. In another case a man was fined for wrongfully detaining on Kent Island two fugitive servants.[5] A third case was one of disputed title to a servant between Edward Hodgkeys and Captain Fendall,[6] and in a fourth Durand was granted an order for a boy, Fendall's property,[7] who had been hired out to a planter and whom Durand claimed by an attachment.

At this term the Commissioners added to the number of their quorum[8] Messrs. Edward Lloyd, Michael Brooke, and John Hatch, as, by "death and absence of some of the Provincial Commissioners of the Quorum, the public affairs of this Province are not so attended" as they ought to be. During the last months of the Puritan regime the Provincial Court met at Patuxent,[9] their capital, on November 3 and 4, December 5,[10] 29, 30, and 31, January 1 and 30, and February 16, 17, and 18, always under Preston's presidency.

In November[11] a case of pretended marriage and other

---

[1] 10 Md. Arch., Prov. Ct., 528, 555.
[2] By some neglect of the defendant for want of delivery, after he had sold her to the plaintiff, 10 Md. Arch., Prov. Ct., 546, 552.
[3] 10 Md. Arch., Prov. Ct., 526.
[4] 10 Md. Arch., Prov. Ct., 521.
[5] 10 Md. Arch., Prov. Ct., 523.
[6] 10 Md. Arch., Prov. Ct., 527, see 560.
[7] 10 Md. Arch., Prov. Ct., 534.
[8] 10 Md. Arch., Prov. Ct., 529.
[9] 10 Md. Arch., Prov. Ct., 549, 554.
[10] 10 Md. Arch., Prov. Ct., 565.
[11] 10 Md. Arch., Prov. Ct., 549; bond 564, deed of cattle 565, receipts 563, discharges 564, mortgage 564, deed of mare 563, earmark

immorality stands out among the usual suits for debt[1] and the other petty entries. The court showed that it would uphold its dignity by fining a man for being drunk in court and another for being a common drunkard, as was shown by his being drunk for three days together, and for "several times profanely swearing in court."[2] At the December court a nuncupative will was accepted,[3] a servant assigned,[4] and four others shipped to Preston were refused by him.[5] The Jew doctor, Jacob Lumbrozo,[6] appeared in the court. A servant petitioned for his freedom, and a planter sued another because he did not sell him as strong a servant as he promised. In another case the hire of a servant by one man to another was disputed. Everywhere we see how important a part of the Provincial social life was the indentured service system.[7] Captain Mitchell appeared as an attorney, and it was objected that he was not qualified by the Statute of 3 James I, ch. 7, the first exact reference I have found to any particular English statute. The case was postponed until March and Mitchell was told he would not be accepted as an attorney before that date. In January, among a number of contract cases, we find two

---

563, deed of land 562, attachment 558, estate of Robert Parr 554 (see 1 Md. Arch., Ass., 362), and of John Drueman 556. He was a merchant, and in January, 1657/8, there were many suits instituted concerning his estate.

[1] 10 Md. Arch., Prov. Ct., 552, 556, 561 (jury trial, which was unusual), 559.
[2] 10 Md. Arch., Prov. Ct., 556, 558.
[3] Basil Little's estate, 10 Md. Arch., Prov. Ct., 565.
[4] 10 Md. Arch., Prov. Ct., 568.
[5] 10 Md. Arch., Prov. Ct., 567. Earmark recorded and sale of heifer on p. 568. Estates coming before the court are those of John Cockerell, Richard Moore and Paul Simpson and —— Dammarell, January 26, 1657/8.
[6] J. H. Hollander, "Some Unpublished Material Relating to Dr. Jacob Lumbrozo, of Maryland," Publications of the American Jewish Historical Society, no. 1.
[7] See Bruce, "Economic and Social Life of Virginia in the Seventeenth Century," in The South in the Building of the Nation, I, 47.

On January 26, 1657/8, Thomas Stone freed Solomon Barbarah from service due Capt. Wm. Stone, excepting the clause that he leave Stone one half his estate on his death, upon payment of four thousand pounds of tobacco.

depositions of interest, showing that one man agreed to take all the other's property and in return therefor maintain him for life "in meat, drink, apparel, and lodging." There is a rather touching series of depositions as to the nuncupative will of one Thomas White, who said that he would leave all his property to Margaret, William Marshall's maid, as they had "past their faith and troth together."

INDEX

Acts of assembly (1650), 27-35; (1650/1), 48; (1654), 80-84; (1657), 110-112; (1658), 115-116.
Adams, Thomas, 74.
"Additional Brief Narrative," 85. *See also* Heamans, Roger.
Anne Arundel County, 11, 29 (and note), 44, 82.
Arley, Thomas, *see* Orley.
Arundel, Lady Anne, 17.
Ashcombe, John, 102.
Assemblies (1650) 17-36; (1650/1), 47-48; (1654), 79-84; (1657), 110-112.
"Babylon's Fall in Maryland," 85. *See also* Strong, Leonard.
Baltimore County, 69.
Banks, Richard, 57, 59, 102.
Barber, Luke, 89, 90 (note), 92, 100 (and note), 107, 108 (note), 110.
Barton, William, 109 (note).
Batten, William, 69.
Battle of the Severn, 97-99, 111.
Beane, Walter, 18 (note).
Belcher, Thomas, 75.
Bennett, Richard, 10, 11, 53-61, 77-79, 105-106, 107-108, 114.
Berkeley, Sir William, 10, 49, 56.
Berry, James, 79 (note), 160.
Besson, Thomas, 110, 111-112.
Bestone, Thomas, 99.
Boulton, Anne, 40, 43.
Boundary of Maryland and Virginia, 51-52, 142.
Bozman, John L. (quoted), 10, 15, 16, 28 (note), 32 (note), 33, 35 (note), 37 (note), 48, 51 (notes), 52 (note), 58 (note), 60, 65 (note), 67 (notes), 69 (note), 73 (note), 74, 79 (note), 80, 81, 92 (note), 97, 98 (note), 108, 109, 111 (note), 113 (note).
Bramhall, William, 160.

Brent, Mrs. Margaret, 45.
Brent, Mrs. Mary, 46 (and note).
Bretton, William, 18.
Brick-making, 144-145.
Brooke, Francis, 18 (note), 27 (note), 43.
Brooke, Michael, 110, 112, 171.
Brooke, Robert, 37-38, 39, 57, 59, 70, 76.
Brough, William, 18 (note).
Brown, John, 99.
Browne, William Hand (quoted), 35 (note), 73 (note), 116.
Bruce, Philip A. (quoted), 14 (note).
Bump, C. W., 69 (note).
Burgess, William, 99.
Calvert, Cecilius (Lord Baltimore), 13-14, 15, 17, 21-24, 35-38, 39, 44, 46, 48-53, 54, 61-65, 76, 89, 106-109, 112-114, 115, 116.
Calvert, Leonard, 21, 22.
Calvert, Philip, 109 (and note), 110, 112, 113, 114.
Calvert County, 76.
Catlyn, Henry, 44.
Cattle, 22, 23, 30, 45-47, 133-134.
Chalmers, George (quoted), 97 (note).
Chandler, Job, 47, 57, 66, 73, 79-80, 99, 107, 161.
Charles County, 38, 39, 76.
Civil War (1654), 84-101.
Claiborne, William, 28, 46-47, 53-61, 77-79.
Clarke, Robert, 24 (and note), 50, 69 (and note), 73, 99, 112-113, 161 (and note).
Collett, Richard, 76, 102.
Commissioners of Parliament, 53-61, 77-84.
Conditions of Plantation, 15-16.
Copley, Father Thomas, 103.
Corbyn, Henry, 100.
Corn, cultivation of, 70.

Index.

Cornwallis, Thomas, 66, 70, 113, 114.
Cornwallis v. Gerard, 141–142.
Cornwallis v. Sterman, 141.
Counties, 11, 29 (and note), 37 (note), 38 (and note), 39, 44, 76, 82.
Coursey, Henry, 92, 101, 108 (note).
Coursey (De Courcy), John, 104.
Coxe, James, 18 (and note).
Cromwell, Oliver, 105–106, 107.
Crouch, Ralph, 99.
Curtis, Edmund, 55–61.
Cutts, John, 99.
Dandy, Anne, 170.
Dandy, John, 161, 168–170.
Davenant, Sir William, 12.
De Courcy, John, see Coursey, John.
Dennis, Robert, 53–61.
Dent, Thomas, 104 (note).
Digges, Edward, 113 (and note).
Divorce, 165–166.
Dobb, John, 104.
Durand, William, 10, 11, 78, 79, 91, 99.
Durford, John, 32.
Eltonhead, Edward, 112.
Eltonhead, William, 38, 39, 89, 91, 94, 99 (and note), 100.
Eltonhead, Mrs. William, 108.
Evans, William, 99–100, 102, 161.
Ewen, William, 79 (note), 161, 164.
Ewens, Richard, 79, 99, 110, 111–112.
Fendall, Josias, 91, 94, 100, 105, 106–110, 112–115.
Fenwick, Cuthbert, 18 (note), 19, 25, 26 (note), 28 (note), 30, 41.
Franklin, Robert, 111.
Fruit culture, 104, 121 (note), 134.
Fuller, William, 59, 66, 67–68, 79, 91, 92, 93, 99, 103, 114.
Gerard, Thomas, 70, 107.
Gibbons, Edward, 47.
Gillett, Augustin, 69.
Godson, Peter, 155, 159.
Golden Fortune, 89.
Golden Lion, 89, 92–98, 100.
Greene, Thomas, 12, 13, 14, 18 (note), 19, 31 (note), 36, 44, 118.
Gwyther, Nicholas, 43, 99, 101, 120 (note), 125 (note), 126.
Hall, Edward, 104.
Hammond, John, 10, 55 (note), 85–86, 87–88, 90, 92 (note), 93 (note), 96 (note), 97 (note), 98–99, 100 (and note).
"Hammond versus Heamans," 86, 89. *See also* Hammond, John.
Harrison, Thomas, 10.
Hatch, John, 18 (note), 79, 101, 171.
Hatton, Thomas, 11, 13, 18 (note), 20, 25, 40 (note), 41, 42, 44, 46, 48, 57–58, 66, 75, 79–80, 98, 103 (and note).
Hatton, Mrs. Thomas, 108.
Hatton, William, 104 (note).
Hawkins, Matthew, 44.
Hawkins, Thomas, 104.
Heamans, Roger, 85, 92–100.
Hely, Abraham, 93, 100.
Hinson, Thomas, 79 (note).
Hodgkeys, Richard, 101, 111.
Homewood, James, 44.
Husbands, Richard, 44 (note).
Indians, 29, 33–34, 45 (and note), 50–51, 59, 60–61, 65–68, 70–71, 74, 83.
Ingle, Richard, 16, 32.
Janson, Abraham, 23, 118–119.
Jarboe, John, 37 (and note), 161.
Jesuits, 14–15, 64, 103–104.
Johnson, James, 110.
Johnson, Peter, 101.
"Just and Cleere Refutation," 86–87. *See also* Langford, John.
Kadger, Robert, 40 (note).
Land, Philip, 126.
Land grants, 14–15, 39, 51, 68–69, 108, 109, 112.
Langford, John, 10, 35 (notes), 57–58, 86–87, 108 (note).
Lawson, John, 79 (note), 101.
"Leah and Rachel," 10–11, 87–88, 89. *See also* Hammond, John.
Leeds, William, 104.
Leggat, John, 100.

Index.   177

Lewger, John, 11, 22.
Lewis, William, 37, 100.
Lewis, Mrs. William, 108.
Lloyd, Edward, 44, 48, 59, 68–69, 76–77, 79, 114, 171.
Lombard, Thomas, 104.
"The Lord Baltimore's Case," 61–64.
McMahon, John V. L. (quoted), 107 (note).
Manners, George, 18 (note), 117.
Marsh, Thomas, 59, 104, 157.
Maryland, conditions in, 1649–1650, 9–17; assembly of 1650, 17–36; proprietor and colonists, 1650–1651, 36–48; the proprietor's instructions of 1651, 48–53; commissioners of Parliament of 1651, 53–61; the proprietor's struggle in England to retain his province, 61–65; Governor Stone, 1652–1653, 65–72; Stone's breach with the commissioners, 72–84; the Maryland civil war, 1654, 84–101; conditions after the war, 101–106; Josias Fendall, Governor, 1656, 106–112; restoration of proprietary government, 1657, 112–116; proceedings of Provincial Court, 1649–1658, 117–173.
Matthews, Samuel, 62, 72, 107–108, 112, 113–114.
Matthews, Thomas, 18 (note), 19–20, 161.
Mears, Thomas, 44, 99, 114, 157.
Medley, John, 18 (note), 26 (note).
Merryman, James, 44.
Metcalf, John, 37, 102–103, 143 (note).
Mitchell, William, 38, 39–43, 52.
Morgan, Philip, 110, 164.
Neill, Edward D. (quoted), 99 (note).
Oath of allegiance to Lord Baltimore, 34–35, 82.
Orley (Arley), Thomas, 104–105.
Oversey, Simon, 72.
Owen, Richard, 95.
Owens, Richard, 69.

Pakes, Walter, 13.
Patuxent County, 82.
Pedro, John, 100.
Pile, John, 18 (note), 161.
Poor laws, 30.
Posey, Francis, 18 (note).
Pott, John, 158.
Potter, Henry, 104.
Preston, Richard, 57, 59, 67, 70, 77, 79 (and note), 91, 110, 114.
Price, John, 18 (note), 25, 26, 57, 59, 65, 66, 99, 107, 160–161.
Protestants, 18–19, 24 (note), 25, 35. *See also* Puritans.
Provincial Court, proceedings of (1649–1658), 117–173.
Puddington, George, 11, 18 (note), 44.
Puritans, 9–11, 15, 35 (and note), 48–49, 62 (and note), 64–65, 67–68, 73, 76–77, 81, 84–85, 91–101, 113.
Randall, D. R. (quoted), 12 (note), 97 (note).
Randall, J. W. (quoted), 11, 98 (and note).
Rapiar, George, 144.
Rents, collection of, 15, 140.
Robins, Robert, 18 (note).
Roman Catholics, 18–19, 24 (note), 26, 64–65, 81.
Scarborough, Edmund, 49.
Servants, 30, 111, 118, 122, 124, 131, 133, 137–138, 143–144, 154, 167 (and notes), 168, 171, 172 (and note).
Sharp, Peter, 110, 112, 166.
Sherman, Thomas, 18 (note).
Sixteen laws, Lord Baltimore's, 21–14, 25, 27, 31–36.
Skinner, Andrew, 110.
Sly, John, 101.
Sly, Robert, 101, 110 (and note).
Smith, John, 79, 101.
Smith, Richard, 99.
Smith, William, 40–41, 42 (and note).
Sparrow, Thomas, 69.
Stagg, Thomas, 53–61.
Starkey, Father Lawrence, 103.
Sterman, John, 84 (note).
Stockbridge, Henry (quoted), 45 (note).
Stockley, Woodman, 158.

Stone, Virlinda, 100.
Stone, William, 9, 12, 13–15, 17–18, 20, 25, 26, 29 (note), 30 (and note), 36, 44–45, 56, 57–59, 65, 67–79, 89–101, 104, 107, 114, 159–160.
Strong, Leonard, 10, 59, 62 (note), 79, 85, 91, 92 (note), 95 (note), 96 (note), 98 (note), 99 (note), 100.
Taxes, 27, 32–33, 83, 111.
Taylor, Robert, 110, 160.
Thomas, Philip, 114, 164.
Thomas, Thomas, 69, 99, 164.
Thompson, William, 66.
Thomson, George, 108 (note), 109 (note).
Thorowgood, Captain, 100, 104 (note).
Thurston, Richard, 17.
Tilghman, Samuel, 89–90, 100.
Tobacco, cultivation of, 70.
Trade, 33–34, 54, 70, 74.
Trueman, Thomas, 108 (note), 109 (note).
Tunnell, Thomas, 102, 109 (note).
Turner, Arthur, 79 (note), 80.
Tyler, Moses Coit (quoted), 87–88.
Underhill, John, 111.

Vaughan, Robert, 18 (and notes), 24 (note), 25, 44 (note), 59, 68–69, 110.
Veitch, James, 162.
Vethers, Samuel, 164.
"Virginia and Maryland," 62 (note), 64–65, 73 (note), 84.
Virginia, relations with, 9–10, 14 (note), 16, 49, 51–52, 53–56, 61–62, 65, 142, 146, 171.
Wade, John, 79 (note), 80.
Walcott, John, 111.
Waring, Sampson, 79 (note), 99, 101, 158, 162.
Warren, Mrs. Susan, 41–42, 43 (note).
Watson, William, 104.
Webber, Thomas, 72.
Weekes, Joseph, 79, 110, 111–112.
Wells, Richard, 79.
Whitlock, Bulstrode, 107.
Whittle, George, 111.
Widdrington, Sir Thomas, 107.
Wilkinson, Rev. William, 42, 104 (and note).
Winchester, John, 104.
Windham, Edward, 57, 59.
Withers, Samuel, 114.
Woolman, Richard, 164.
Yardley, Francis, 57, 59, 66, 74 (and note).